X II

Domination or Liberation

DOMINATION
— OR —
LIBERATION

The Place of Religion in Social Conflict

ALISTAIR KEE

SCM PRESS LTD

British Library Cataloguing-in-Publication Data available

334 00330 X

First published 1986
by SCM Press Ltd
26–30 Tottenham Road, London N1

Typeset at The Spartan Press Ltd,
Lymington, Hants
and printed in Great Britain by
Billing & Sons Ltd
Worcester

To the Memory of my Parents
Robert Kee
Agnes Stevenson Kee

Contents

Introduction

The chapters of this book are a slightly enlarged version of the Ferguson Lectures, delivered at the University of Manchester in February, 1986. Before introducing the subject I wish to express my thanks to the University for the invitation to undertake the series, to the Faculty of Theology for the generous spirit in which they responded to the lecture material, and especially to Professor A. O. Dyson for his encouragement and kindness during my residence. The general field of the Ferguson Lectures is 'Christianity in the Modern World'; far from being restrictive, such guidelines invite consideration of some of the most important and exciting developments which have taken place in the history of the Christian religion. If we take 'modern' to mean not Descartes in the seventeenth century or Schleiermacher in the nineteenth, but the decades through which many of us have actually lived, then the central feature of the story must be the impact which certain new and profound movements within society have had upon religious thought and experience. The generic term for these movements has been 'liberation'. Thus the women's movement has sought liberation from sexual oppression. The black movement has worked to end racial oppression. And in the Third World, especially in Latin America but also in Africa and Asia, there have been many groups working for political, economic and cultural liberation. Each of these has impacted on Christian thought and practice; or, more correctly, Christians involved in such movements have reflected on their traditions in the light of new experiences and perspectives. If the movements have been for liberation, then what they have sought to expose and overcome can be called 'domination'. Thus women involved in the feminist movement have been able to identify and reject the many forms in which sexual domination is expressed in society. And Christian feminists have additionally been forced to ask about the part which religion has played in such domination and the contribution which it might make towards liberation. The articulation of these matters has become known as feminist theology. This will be the subject of the first chapter. In chapters 2 and 3 we shall be examining black theology and liberation theology.

Although I shall be viewing each movement sympathetically as it attempts to overcome domination and establish liberation, I shall be critical of specific writers, or their assumptions and goals. Indeed there will be evidence of a running tension amongst the three movements. Theo Witvliet, the Dutch theologian, has pointed to some examples during meetings of the Ecumenical Association of Third World Theologians. At their meeting in Detroit in 1975 'the Latin Americans present had to cope with the criticism that their Marxist class analysis did not do justice to the distinctive underivable dynamics of racism and sexism'.[1] A serious criticism, especially when there are, for example, more black people in Brazil than in the whole of the USA. But at the same time Allan Boesak, the coloured South African theologian, criticizes any American black theologian who makes 'his own situation (being black in America) and his own movement (liberation from white racism) the ultimate criterion of theology'.[2] And if black theology, at least to begin with, paid little attention to sexual domination, feminist theologians must now come to terms with a fundamental narrowness in their perception of the world. This has been belatedly recognized by Carter Heyward. 'While few, if any, of us white women intended to exclude the lives of women of colour from our concerns, we simply had not begun to comprehend the extent to which women of different racial/ethnic groups have disparate historical and contemporary experiences of sexism.'[3] Liberation is largely defined by the domination which it opposes, and it would appear that those who suffer under one form of domination may themselves be responsible for imposing another form of domination on some other group.

This would suggest that domination cannot be successfully attacked or eliminated piecemeal, because its various forms are interrelated. Indeed it would further suggest that domination is more than the sum of its instances, and that it could usefully be regarded as an ideology. As a world-view or mind-set involving assumptions about power, privilege, interest and advantage it promotes a picture of social relations as entirely natural. Whether it be relations between the sexes, the races or the classes, the ideology of domination explains in a plausible way why how things are is how they should be. It is for this reason that religion has been such an important factor in constructing and maintaining the ideology. As Peter Berger points out, 'Religion has been the historically most widespread and effective instrument of legitimation. All legitimation maintains socially defined reality. Religion legitimates so effectively because it relates the precarious reality constructions of empirical societies with ultimate reality.'[4] Liberation therefore begins with suspicion, the raising of a question about what was previously taken for granted. Is it really the case that one group should occupy a position of superiority with respect to another? Are the grounds as objective as we have always been led to believe? Christians who are alive to domination and take up the cause of liberation must, in addition to everything else, examine the part which their religion has played in the legitimation of domination in the spheres of gender, race, class, politics and economics. More positively, they must consider how religion, freed from its associations with domination, might contribute to liberation.

I shall therefore criticize liberation theologians if they concern themselves exclusively with one form of domination, ignoring other forms and the extent to which their progress might be at the expense of other groups. But I shall be making a more important criticism, which will emerge in the course of the book and which can be introduced here only in summary form. Domination causes suffering and humiliation, and it is entirely proper that those who promote liberation are motivated by a certain righteous anger against specific cases of domination. Domination has practical consequences and is not a matter merely for reflection. And yet, as with any other social phenomenon, it is as well to have an accurate understanding of it through some form of critical theory. I am suggesting here that domination cannot be overcome solely by attacking its many instances. It has to be understood as an ideology which hides behind accepted values and respected institutions. While righteous anger is proper as a motive, it provides no critical theory. On occasion I shall therefore criticize a certain naivety amongst liberation theologians, especially when they adopt a moralistic approach to domination. Denouncing specific instances of domination will do nothing to end domination; it will only produce alternative forms. Cutting the heads off weeds actually stimulates the roots to produce new outcrops. But there is still a more important matter which I shall be taking up in the course of the book. Those who lack a critical theory fail to understand that domination is not identical with ill-will. Yes, there are many instances in which evil people dominate whenever they can. Yet as we shall see, a much more serious problem is encountered when we recognize that within a society or institution people of good-will and integrity also dominate. Domination cannot be accounted for simply by accusing them of hypocrisy. If only that were the case! The ideology runs so deeply that in many cases those who have no intention of dominating nevertheless continue oppression. In the most extreme cases such people oppress even groups and individuals towards whom they are actually well-disposed. But more of this as we proceed.

The subject of the book should now be clear. It concerns the part which religion plays in three areas of social conflict: gender, race and class. The options are domination or liberation. A pattern will emerge in the first three chapters. Religion will be seen to have legitimized domination in the past, justifying domination and providing it with moral authority and social status. Indeed, as we shall see, religion has even added its own specific forms of domination. But in each case we shall consider the ways in which Christianity in the modern world has helped to expose this role, and has begun the transformation by which religion might now actually begin to contribute to liberation in each of these spheres. The pattern is therefore of a movement from domination to liberation. As the reader will now begin to suspect, this is not the end of the story. If the first three chapters deal with liberation movements of the 1960s and 1970s, there is another movement which has appeared in the 1980s. The most recent development is a backlash against liberation. A persistent theme of liberation theologies has been exodus, how God leads the oppressed (women, blacks, poor) out of cruel and unjustified bondage. As one white Anglo-Saxon Protestant American complained: 'In all their exoduses and liberation plots, I'm Pharaoh.'[5] Women invariably say that working for a woman boss is worse than working for a man. Blacks in Africa have, on independence, practised their own racism, instituting persecution on the basis of tribalism. And even Marx observed that some forms of communism were motivated by envy and greed. The New Right in America and neo-conservatism in Britain have had enough of guilt and now wish to stand up for the things in which they have always believed, though until recently they did not dare to advocate them publicly. The governments of Reagan and Thatcher have undertaken many legislative initiatives, but it is important not to lose sight of the wood for the trees. Their most important achievement has been to call into question the assumptions undergirding the consensus society produced in the last two decades. They will be remembered above all for changing the ethos of both countries. The political Right has won the battle (and who cares about the argument?). Those who speak today of liberation sound like hippies caught in a time warp. The new macho language is of initiative, self-reliance, competition, and the entrepreneurial instinct. As Rodney Bickerstaffe said at the Labour Party Conference in 1985, it is the argument that to get the rich to work harder you must pay them more, while to get the poor to work harder, you must pay them less. There is no talk of liberation, and there is much evidence of the reimposition of domination by gender, race and class. The question which we shall take up in the last chapter is therefore whether this movement of domination can count on religion once again for legitimation. The era of liberation was exciting and hopeful. It may now have come to an end. At the very least this would be disappointing. But the American theologian Richard Shaull reads the signs of the times differently and comes to the following chilling conclusion:

> Sooner or later, we may face here a situation similar to that which confronted German Christians in the time of Hitler. The struggle between repressive religion – allied with repressive political forces – and transformative faith is essentially a struggle about what belief in and obedience to Jesus Christ are about in this time and place.[6]

one

Religion and the
Domination of Women

I wish to begin by assuring feminists that this title does not indicate a
How-To chapter. I am not going to show how it is possible to dominate
women by use of religion, but rather to show how it has been done in the
past, and to some extent in the present, in the hope that now that it is
exposed as an ideology, as a form of false consciousness, it will lose its
former justification and legitimacy. I begin with this area of domination
first of all because it is the most extensive, running throughout recorded
human history, across most if not all known societies, and directly
affecting more than half of the world's population. Domination on the
basis of gender is so pervasive because it is present everywhere in
addition to all other forms of domination. Thus white people may seek
to dominate black people, using race as the occasion of domination, but
black men can also dominate black women. Rich people can dominate
poor people, using economics as the occasion, but poor men can still
dominate poor women. It is also appropriate to begin with this area,
because in the history of Europe religion has been the most important
factor in promoting and maintaining the domination of women.

The unmasking of the ideology of domination has been performed by
the feminist movement. It is feminist consciousness which has drawn to
our attention the fact that the place and role of women in society is not
natural, but is rather the result of a social construction. I had originally
prepared as an introduction to this lecture a series of brief assessments
of some leading feminist writers, but such is the volume of material on
women and religion that it is not possible to begin so far back. In any case
the main features of feminist consciousness will be familiar. For
example there is the critique of the dependence in which women have
lived, so that they do not live their own lives, but must look to men for

food and shelter. There is the critique of the consequent immaturity of such a relationship, in which even adult women are not free and responsible for their lives. These two themes are prominent in the work of Betty Friedan.[1] In the more philosophical analysis of Simone de Beauvoir the critique is that women are made objects within men's lives, that women are not subjects at the centre of their own worlds.[2] De Beauvoir also brings out the consequence of this situation, that women lose the sense of solidarity with other women that might be expected from common oppression. As an existentialist she makes a good deal of the tension which women experience between the freedom of human nature and the biological determinism of the life of nature. The work of Kate Millett, by contrast, examines the political setting, providing a theory of patriarchy in which relationships within the family are projected on to the larger institutions of society. Women are trapped within the family and have only a mediated relationship to the world of industry, commerce or indeed the state at large.[3]

I therefore propose to approach the subject of the domination of women through a series of studies done by feminist writers. I shall make some critical comments along the way, but we shall see an emerging picture of the way in which religion has been used to dominate women. We shall also see elements which have contributed or could contribute to the liberation of women. Before I begin, however, I wish to make a distinction which I think is important in dealing with this material, but which is not made by the writers themselves. It will be important to distinguish between two different sources of domination. The first is what might be called 'conventional' domination. The term is not used to excuse or to minimize this discrimination, for in practice it causes the same suffering and humiliation as any other kind. Rather, it is used to draw attention to the fact that in some cultures at various periods men might dominate women because that is the way things have always been. It is always possible that with changes in the culture, linked perhaps to economic conditions, the customs will change. Thus domination in this conventional sense might be reduced, or pass away. In contrast I wish to draw attention to domination which is raised to the level of a moral or religious principle. In this case the same changes in culture might take place, the society in other respects might become progressive, enlightened, or liberal, but the domination of women could not change correspondingly, because it is a matter of religious principle. This is an important distinction to make, especially in the modern world. It directly affects the issue of the ordination of women in various churches. But first of all, we should look at a series of historical examples which illustrate, positively and negatively, the relationship between religion and the domination of women.

Feminists have studied the place of women in the Old Testament, in part because attitudes and values passed from Judaism into early Christianity, and in part because the Hebrew scriptures were appropriated by the church and influenced the development of the church in later centuries in specific circumstances. Phyllis Bird has written on 'Images of Women in the Old Testament' (= *SR*).[4] Her treatment of the material is not only of a high level of historical-critical scholarship, but it displays the perspective and sensitivity of feminist consciousness. That is to say, it is not a simple rehearsal of some central passages in which women are mentioned. Rather, we see in the presentation some of the themes already noted in secular writers. Thus she claims that 'the Old Testament is a collection of writings by males from a society dominated by males' (*SR*, 41). Women appear in the Old Testament only in relation to men and to the activities of men. The religion of the Old Testament is not only a male religion, but consequently God is conceived of in male terms, and is concerned for the most part with males. Thus women are marginalized in both respects. I wish to divide the material in a way quite different from that of Bird.

Although the Old Testament is a collection of religious books, not everything included is specifically religious. Bird deals with the place of women in the historical works and in the wisdom literature. For the most part the material she surveys describes the place of women in Jewish society at different times. They are clearly discriminated against, but the discrimination is of that type which I have called conventional. That is to say, it derives from social attitudes and customs and could conceivably change without any matter of principle being challenged.

In Proverbs woman is not referred to simply in terms of biology or property. She appears in more social contexts, making a more complex series of contributions. However, these contributions are still in relation to males. She is a mother who can provide wisdom and guidance for her son, especially in his relations with women. She is a wife who by her demeanour and actions can be of positive value to her husband. She can take initiatives, within the household or even in business. Her actions and character redound to her husband's benefit. She is a wise women, but quite asexual. It is as the other woman, the harlot, that woman uses her sexuality to lead men astray. Such women are outwith the control of men. They may be independent, but they are not wise or positive.

In the historical books there are a very few women who are the subjects of the narratives, notably Deborah and Jezebel; for the most part women appear as the wife/mother. Lesser categories, such as the barren woman, the foreign woman and the widow, are categories related to the main roles. The wife/mother is normally compassionate, subject to suffering, not least at childbirth, often troubled and insecure. Her security within marriage is related to bearing children, and if she does not bear children then she has not only failed her husband, but is considered rejected by God. The childless women was also deprived of the only relationship in which a woman might legitimately have power over another person. As a wife/mother she had status, honour and also authority, being expected to nurture and teach and guide her children. Yet even this was within the veto of her husband. Bird suggests that for all the variations there is a composite picture of women in the historical books. 'She is intelligent, beautiful, discreet, and loyal to her husband . . . Prudent, quick-witted and resourceful, she is capable of independent action, but always acts in her husband's behalf. The good wife does not attempt to rule her husband, nor does she openly oppose him. She defers to him in speech and action, obeys his wish as his command, and puts his welfare first. She employs her sexual gifts for his pleasure alone and raises up children to his name' (*SR*, 65). Marriages were arranged between families, and the terminology used indicates the active role of the male and the relative passivity of the female. Her treatment was to some extent dependent on the family from which she came, and on whether it had the power to ensure her fair treatment. By the same token woman is always an alien within the household, having continuing links with another family and even another nation. But between the two male institutions she was not independent. In the historical works women are involved in serious matters. They can be loyal or traitorous, they can be generous or scheming, but they are not sexual objects. As Bird concludes, 'Women may be portrayed as unscrupulous, but they are rarely, if ever, characterized as foolish' (*SR*, 70). They make an impact for good or ill, but always within a male world.

Even within the apodictic laws the discrimination could still be reckoned as conventional. The context of the Ten Commandments is clearly male. 'You shall be men consecrated to me' (Ex. 22.31). Men are the subjects who are addressed and religious obligations are theirs. The last of the Ten Commandments discloses this perspective. 'Thou shalt not covet thy neighbour's house, thou shalt not covet thy neighbour's wife, nor his manservant, nor his maidservant, nor his ox, nor his ass, nor anything that is thy neighbour's.' The placing of women higher up the list than the ox and ass, though not so high as the house, hardly compensates for their being on such a list in the first place. However, this is convention, and though by modern standards it is perhaps thoughtless or insensitive, no cosmic principle is involved and with a change in attitudes the commandments have been accepted as being addressed also to women. Laws about adultery were very strict, but at that time this was because they were in fact concerned with property and theft. Thus in extramarital sex, if the woman was not married, no theft had taken place. If the woman was married, then the property of the husband had been misappropriated. The jealous God will not share his people with the gods, and the religion of Israel was distinguished from many of the neighbouring cults by its elimination of sex. Thus, as Bird points out, 'Sexual offenses are religious offenses in Israel' (*SR*, 78).

However, the images of women in the more specifically religious context are very different. The ritual laws in particular defined uncleanness in ways which made it very difficult for women to participate in the cult for most of their adult lives. The discriminatory nature of these laws can be exemplified in the distinction that a woman was ritually unclean for a week after the birth of a son, but unclean for two weeks in the case of a daughter. It is in this ritual definition that we see discrimination against women raised to a religious principle. No social changes are relevant to this principle of the inferiority of women. We see an instance of this in the days of King David, when he requests some bread for his soldiers from the priest at Nob. The priest has only the bread from the sanctuary, which he will give to them if he can be assured on only one matter: 'I have no common bread at hand, but there is holy bread; if only the young men have kept themselves from women' (I Sam. 21.4). The contrast is between that which is holy and any contact with women. Of course the standard of evaluation has nothing to do with morality. Contact with women will defile them. This was the kind of point that a religious specialist would make, and it is noticeable that such questions were not determinative of the position of women in the life of society, as we have seen. The same is true also of the most famous passage on the subject of women, namely the creation account of Adam and Eve, in Genesis 2–3. Although this has proved fascinating for European history, it seems to have had little impact on the social life of Israel. Eve, for example, is never again mentioned in the Old Testament. But the passage has been very influential on Christian thinking and therefore on the development of European attitudes towards women, outwith Judaism. It must be said that in this account of creation, the Almighty seems to be making it up as he goes along. He has created the heaven and earth, vegetation and rivers to form a garden, and then man, in this case Adam. In the apodictic tradition the commandment about the tree is given to man alone. To keep Adam company God creates the animals and birds. It is man's world, and he names all things. So that when God decides that this is still not enough and that man should have a companion not of the beasts but of his own flesh, Eve is created into Adam's world. This kind of situation is important for existentialist writers, and when Bird comes to describe it, her presentation is similar to the work of de Beauvoir. 'With the creation of woman, man is finally his true self, a sexual social being.' 'She is the "thou" that confronts him and the other that completes him' (*SR*, 73). Bird probably goes too far in seeing the J account as asserting the equality of man and woman: the story makes the existence of woman derivative and existentially dependent. But she makes an important point in saying that marriage thus enables man to achieve the reunion of his own flesh (*SR*, 87). Sexuality is not a source of evil, but an expression of God's original intention that man and woman should share a common life. But if everything in the garden was rosy, the point of the story is not to describe a primordial state, but to explain the present condition of the world. Working back, we can say that since this world is full of suffering and misfortune, and since on the writer's view such things are sent as punishment by God, then the conclusion must be that it all stems from a primordial sin. And since women are the source of temptation and trouble, as we have seen, then the primordial offence must have been committed by Eve, though Adam was subsequently drawn into the guilt and certainly the consequences. Bird would therefore like to draw the conclusion that woman was not intended to be dominated by man, but in this I think she fails to understand the point of the story. Woman was intended to occupy a place within man's world. That is the general male perspective of the Old Testament, and it would lead to what we have called conventional discrimination. But Bird completely omits any discussion of the specific consequences of the Fall. Adam and Eve are affected by the Fall, but in quite different ways. Adam, now mortal, will find that life is no bed of roses, but the consequences for Eve are threefold. First, she will suffer great pain in childbirth. Secondly, she will have strong sexual desires for her husband. Thirdly, 'he shall rule over you'. Thus not only is woman reduced to her biological, sexual roles, but she must be dominated by man. Or, to return to the function of the story, the domination of woman by man is now raised to a religious and cosmic principle. It matters not whether it was the original intention of God or not; in this world man has a religious duty to dominate woman. Before leaving this account we might note that feminists derive some pleasure from the fact that Eve is portrayed as intelligent, enquiring, capable of initiative and having the capacity to make aesthetic judgments. Adam by contrast is a real wally, dull, inept, quick to pass the buck, passive, easily led and readily accepting of whatever is served up for his dinner.

Notwithstanding the fact that Eve seems like a much more interesting person than Adam, the upshot of the J narrative is to justify the subordination of women to men in all circumstances. This is a religious principle, and is not subject to modification through social change. There is, however, another account of the creation which gives a completely different image of women. It is strange that, as the first chapter of the entire Bible, it has had so little impact on Jews or Christians. It is either ignored in favour of the more exotic account in chapters 2 and 3, 'Former Garden Girl Tells All', or more often recalled in the context of the second account. It is worth noting that the account in chapter 1 is by a priestly source, and might therefore have been expected to give a predominantly male-orientated narrative. But this is not the case. The story does not seem to be describing society as it is or attempting to justify it. It is indicating the true nature of things and man's true life. After everything else has been created and pronounced good, man is created as the last act in this drama. Or rather it is mankind which is created, qualitatively distinct from the rest of creation. 'So God created man in his own image, in the image of God he created him; male and female he created them.' They are to procreate, and this too will be pronounced good. They are to have dominion over everything else, but neither man nor woman is to have domination over the other. The passage is too cryptic for us to be certain what constitutes the image of God. Under the male perspective this question has normally been discussed as if God were a very large man. However, in the feminist perspective it would seem that androgyny was the characteristic of what God has created: mankind is male and female together. It certainly does not mean that there is no difference between man and woman. Precisely the opposite. But it does indicate that only in a non-dominating relationship can man and woman attain true life. Here marriage is the norm and sexuality is an inherent part of being human. We may therefore conclude that in the Old Testament, apart from a conven-

tional and therefore corrigible male domination, there are two tendencies specifically related to religion. The first is the view that women are
inferior to men and that man has a religious duty to control woman.
Sexual relations on this view are evil, since they are a consequence of the
Fall. On the second view man and woman are equal partners in a
relationship. Although the writer knows that people can be evil,
marriage and sexual relations are not sources of evil, nor are they in
themselves expressions of evil. In a world in which the ideology of
domination is rife it was inevitable, but none the less tragic that the
religious legitimation of domination and discrimination against women
should have been more influential, while the egalitarian view, which
could have contributed to liberation from the ideology, seems to have
had so little impact.

I have been suggesting that the influence of the Old Testament could
have been on liberation, but that in fact it has been, at least to date, on
the side of domination. Why was the third chapter of Genesis more
influential than the first? No doubt because those who wished to find a
religious legitimation for what they were already doing found it in
chapter 3. When we turn to the New Testament the same issue is raised,
but more powerfully. As we shall see, the Gospels contain the impulse
towards liberation, and yet they have been ignored in favour of elements
in the Epistles which justify domination. Why should the practice of
Jesus be set aside in favour of the teaching of Paul? Those who read
sought what they wished to use, a weapon against women. One of the
most impressive feminist studies of Christian origins published in the
last few years is by Elizabeth Schüssler Fiorenza, entitled *In Memory of
Her* (= *MH*).[5] I shall follow the argument as presented in that book,
though especially in the treatment of Paul we shall again have to provide
a different setting for the material.

If we were to continue our previous discussion of Adam and Eve into
the Gospels, we should find that feminists take some satisfaction from
how well women come out of the accounts and how badly men are
portrayed. Familiarity with the narratives takes from us the astonish-
ment that would otherwise greet them. As Mark's Gospel comes to a
climax, as the plans are being made to arrest Jesus, and as one of the
disciples is deciding to betray him, the momentum is broken by a
detailed account of an incident in a house at Bethany. To modern
readers the scene is almost slapstick. A women suddenly entered the
room, poured the contents of a jar over the head of the honoured guest,
and left. The incident invites a series of comparisons. The male

disciples of Jesus had earlier discussed whether Jesus was the Messiah, the anointed one, but here in the most practical way comes a woman disciple to anoint him. In the parallel passage in Luke 7, in contrast to those who do not greet Jesus appropriately, the woman takes the humble role of the servant, reminiscent of Jesus washing the feet of his disciples. In Mark the witness of the woman is so expressive of the significance of Jesus that he declares that wherever the gospel is proclaimed this action will be recalled, 'in memory of her'. Of whom? But she was a woman. The names of the betrayer Judas and the forsaker Peter are remembered, but not the name of the woman whose action is to be recalled throughout history. Nor is this an isolated instance. From the exchanges between Elizabeth and Mary to the loyal women at the cross and the resurrection women perceive the deep religious truths of the events surrounding them, to which male society would as a matter of course marginalize them. By comparison the disciples, who are in the most privileged position of all, are repeatedly described throughout the Gospels as not understanding anything about Jesus and his message. 'Beware of the leaven of the Pharisees,' Jesus tells them, but they think he is speaking about a recipe for bread (Matt. 16.6). When we consider the male orientation of the religious and social institutions of the time it is all the more remarkable that women are portrayed with such characteristics of insight and initiative in contrast to men, who seem to be very limited in perception and even in loyalty. Feminist consciousness does not produce new material, but rather provides a perspective from which the familiar looks very different indeed. 'Both Christian feminist theology and biblical interpretation are in the process of rediscovering that the Christian gospel cannot be proclaimed if the women disciples and what they have done are not remembered' (*MH*, xiv).

A feminist reading of the Gospels therefore indicates that women had a special place in what Fiorenza calls 'the Jesus movement'. This fact alone would distinguish it from the many other groups, orthodox and sectarian, within Judaism at that time. Indeed that women had any place at all in the movement would distinguish it. In continuity with the characteristics of the Old Testament to which I have previously referred, we should expect that these groups would be male, attempting to meet the requirements of a patriarchal religion. We should also expect little attention to be given specifically to women who, as we have seen, were not only marginalized in society, but subject to definitions of uncleanness peculiar to women. Therefore although Jesus proclaimed the coming of the Kingdom of God, as did others, 'this future is mediated and promised to all members of Israel. No one is exempted. Everyone is invited. Woman as well as men, prostitutes as well as Pharisees' (*MH*, 121). With this we begin to glimpse the attractiveness of the Jesus movement to women, and why they were able to occupy a place within it denied them in the other groups. Jesus has a special concern for three categories of people. The first is the poor, those singled out in the Beatitudes, many of whom were women and children. The second is the sick. Fiorenza points out the concern for wholeness rather than ritual holiness. The woman with the issue of blood was ill, but socially and religiously she was permanently unclean. Yet Jesus, in healing her, pays no attention to the definition of her uncleanness, which would make him also unclean. Similarly, in healing the daughter of Jairus he touches the girl who, if dead, was also unclean. He is prepared to break the sabbath because it is wholeness that God wishes for his people. The third category of people with whom Jesus is specially concerned is comprised of tax collectors, sinners and prostitutes. They too are welcome, indeed go into the kingdom before the Pharisees. An extraordinary claim!

Fiorenza as a feminist draws attention to the reasons why the Jesus movement would make this special appeal to women, who might otherwise have felt that the kingdom of God was not for them. Which is another way of saying that in the teaching and table fellowship of Jesus there is a new understanding of God. So far we have been confronted by a male view of God, in a patriarchal context. Fiorenza seems to be saying that other characteristics of God are now revealed, and that these are better represented in female language. Although in earlier times prophetic literature, in its condemnation of goddess cults, has eschewed such terms, wisdom literature speaks of the wisdom of God personified as female. 'Goddess language is employed to speak about the one God of Israel whose gracious goodness is divine Sophia' (*MH*, 134). There are a very few places in the Gospels where this female personification of the divine wisdom appears. For example Jesus justifies his association with sinners and his table fellowship. 'Yet wisdom is justified by her deeds' (Matt. 11.19). Fiorenza is arguing for two things at this point. The first is to identify certain aspects of the teaching and associations of Jesus with female roles and attitudes. Thus, Jesus welcomes the heavy laden, 'for I am gentle and lowly of heart' (Matt. 11.29). (Incidentally, in the preceding verses Jesus has been speaking specifically about the Father and the Son.) Another example of the female attitude and role would be Jesus weeping over Jerusalem. 'How often have I wanted to gather your children as a mother bird collects her young under her wings, but you refused me' (Luke 13.34). The second point for which Fiorenza is arguing here is that, 'It was possible to understand Jesus' ministry and death in terms of God-Sophia, because Jesus probably understood himself as the prophet and child of Sophia' (*MH*, 134). Anyone familiar with the Life-of-Jesus research will recognize the temptation to justify a position by identifying it as the self-consciousness of Jesus. However, even without this step Fiorenza is making the important claim that the teaching of Jesus concerning the invitation into the kingdom implies a very different understanding of God. 'The Sophia-God of Jesus does not need atonement or sacrifices. Jesus' death is not willed by God but is the result of his all-inclusive praxis as Sophia's prophet' (*MH*, 135).

The Jesus movement was soon faced with the problem of carrying on and extending this 'all-inclusive praxis'. Although there are signs that Jesus addressed himself primarily to Jews, there are indications in the Gospel of how the church should develop. Thus the Syro-Phoenician woman begs him to exorcize a demon from her daughter (Mark 7.24–30). One aspect of the story particularly pleasing to feminists is that while Jesus initially refuses, the woman proceeds to argue with him and rather neatly turns his argument back till he can only agree to do what she asks. The wisdom of God, which treats women as people in their own right, is incarnate here. In unconcealed delight at the Syro-Phoenician woman, Fiorenza confers upon her the rather over-the-top title of 'apostolic foremother of all gentile Christians' (*MH*, 138). Some have tried to subsume women in the Gospels under the poor and sinners, as if Jesus paid no particular attention to women. Fiorenza argues that Jesus specifically rejected patriarchy because of its nature and associations. Thus he commands his followers to 'call no man your father on earth, for you have one Father, who is in heaven' (Matt. 23.9). In the new egalitarian community women are not to be marginalized, coming to God only through men. But this is a particular instance of the rejection of domination more generally, whether of gender, race, class or age. 'The "father" God is invoked here, however, not to justify patriarchal structures and relationships in the community of disciples but precisely to reject such claims, powers, and structures' (*MH*, 150). The ignoring of this very specific commandment of Jesus represents the re-patriarchalizing of religion in the early church, the legitimizing of domination not only of women, but of the poor and marginalized generally. Fiorenza proceeds to examine material which illustrates this tension within the early church. On the one hand the welcome which Jesus extended to woman and other disadvantaged classes meant that they were free to show initiative and leadership in ways that had been denied to them within Jewish society and especially within Jewish religion. Fiorenza covers this material in some detail. On the other hand many of the leaders of the church were Jewish males who tended to interpret their experience with Jesus in older messianic and patriarchal terms. Paul illustrates this tension in his teaching concerning the place of women in the church. Paul found in Christianity the fulfilment of Pharisaic Judaism, which is another way of saying that he never rejected his earlier religious faith. In contrast to the original disciples Paul had no interest in sectarian Judaism and therefore he does not present the faith in the terms which characterize the Synoptic Gospels. Nor in contrast to his successors did he look to Christianity to provide answers to the metaphysical problems of Greek philosophy or religion. His letters are for the most part practical, dealing with matters of conduct. This is characteristic of the issues covered in I Corinthians. Chapter 7 is one of the central passages quoted by those who regard Paul as a chauvinist who provides material to justify the denigration of women, the dehumanizing of sexuality and the evacuation of any positive significance to marriage even among Christians. Yet Fiorenza, for her own purposes, chooses not to draw any negative conclusions about Paul in this section. Instead she draws attention to two aspects of Paul's teaching which might be regarded positively by women. The first is that Paul separates sexual intercourse from procreation. Relations between men and women are not governed simply by the intention of having children, or by the chance of having them. Also, when Paul advises widows, for example, not to remarry, he is actually establishing the possibility of freedom from control by some male or other. In this Paul was going against Jewish law, Hellenistic custom and, at least in the time of Augustus, against imperial law. A feminist reading of the chapter picks out these positive features. What is more surprising is that Fiorenza chooses to ignore or play down the more obviously negative elements. Indeed the chapter begins with the abrasive assertion: 'It is well for a man not to touch a woman. But because of the temptation to immorality, each man should have his own wife and each woman have her own husband' (I Cor. 7.1, 2). The fact that Paul begins in this way, referring back to previous discussions he has had with the Corinthian church, means that we do not have the context in which to understand his teaching. However, there is no doubt that it opened the door to the repatriarchalizing of religion, promoting the view that sex detracts from the spiritual life, and that women are a source of temptation, and therefore of evil. It is also spoken from a male perspective, and therefore recalls the Adam and Eve relationship. Having control over sexuality, for example being able to abstain for specific periods, seems to have been regarded in the early church as an admirable thing, but Paul goes beyond this and with a rather smug reference to the fact that he is not married, tells his fellow Christians, 'I wish that all were as I myself am' (I Cor. 7.7). This has also been a very important text in the patriarchalizing of the church, but Fiorenza chooses not to make anything of it.

When we turn to I Corinthians 11 we find the same curious procedure: Fiorenza as feminist and scholar is at pains to interpret Paul in such a way as to avoid all patriarchalizing elements. RSV draws verse 1 back into chapter 10, 'Be imitators of me, as I am of Christ.' It may indeed be the conclusion to the teaching in chapter 10, but it is also a bridge to the next chapter. We are presented here with teaching which, if the convoluted arguments are anything to go by, is not entirely convincing, and Paul frequently adds authority to argument. Here he commends his teaching by referring to his own example, and adds the authority that he is following the example of Christ. The issues involved in chapter 10 are peculiar to those living in the Hellenistic culture of the empire at large, so that Paul is not referring to the example of the historical Jesus. This is a theological line of command. This model is further extended in the next two verses. 'I commend you because you remember me in everything and maintain the traditions even as I have delivered them to you. But I want you to understand that the head of every man is Christ, the head of a woman is her husband, and the head of Christ is God' (vv. 2–3). Thus he has filled out the chain of patriarchal command: God, Christ, (Paul,) man, woman. This is a matter so sufficiently important that it can be taken to stand by itself. But Fiorenza refuses to see any patriarchalizing in it, even though it has been an important text in this respect in the subsequent history of the church. In form criticism as in common experience, a train of thought is frequently determined by association of ideas. Paul, having written about heads, now takes up an associated issue. Yes, that reminds me, I meant to raise with you the covering and uncovering of heads during worship. At this point Fiorenza is more convincing, discussing one of the features of such churches, namely the initiative which women prophets took, under the influence of what she frequently calls the Spirit-Sophia. Women, apparently while in ecstatic states, would unbind their hair and present a picture of 'ritual madness'. Paul was concerned not to try to prevent Spirit ecstasy, but to ensure that, especially for outsiders who might be visiting, or new converts, everything was done decently and in good order. Yet this does not account for other statements which Paul makes. 'For a man ought not to cover his head, since he is the image and glory of God; but woman is the glory of man' (I Cor. 11.7). Fiorenza rather desperately claims that this does not deny that woman is made in the image of God. But surely the text does mean the inferiority of woman, the marginalization of woman once again, so that her value and worth are in relation to man? Fiorenza is referring to the P tradition of Genesis, in which man and woman are equally the image of God, but Paul has in mind rather the J narrative, since he goes on immediately to back up his argument with the supernumerary bone tradition. 'For man was not made from woman, but woman from man' (I Cor. 11.8).

When we turn finally to I Corinthians 14 we find the same reticence by Fiorenza. In this chapter Paul is again concerned for order and decency in the Christian assemblies, and in particular comments on the phenomenon of speaking in tongues. He then concludes with the famous passage on women keeping silent. 'As in all the churches of the saints, the women should keep silence in the churches. For they are not permitted to speak, but should be subordinate, as even the law says. If there is anything they desire to know, let them ask their husbands at home. For it is shameful for a woman to speak in church' (v. 33b–35). Fiorenza argues that since Paul did not attempt to prevent women ecstatics when discussing worship in chapter 7, he cannot mean all women must keep silent, only married women. Only married women! But throughout the feminist movement have not married women been regarded as the most oppressed group of all? Is it somehow in Paul's defence that it should be said that he only discriminates against married women? Fiorenza seems pleased that Paul can ascribe 'a special holiness to the unmarried woman and virgin' (*MH*, 231). Given that Paul so often writes from a male perspective it is more likely that he is speaking about women in general, assuming that in general women are married. Although he does not wish to prevent ecstatic women prophesying, Paul is simply saying that in the normal course of things he does not want women speaking or taking leadership roles or showing initiative. Yes, there were examples of female initiative and leadership. Paul knew of them, but still did not like it. A few examples could be absorbed, but he is closing the door to a movement in which ordinary women as a matter of course are equals in the assemblies. Fiorenza quotes Conzelmann with approval, that Paul is here 'taking over bourgeois moral concepts which denote not absolute but conventional values' (*MH*, 231). But she seems somehow reconciled to the marriage patriarchalism of the passage. 'However, the text does not say that wives should subordinate themselves either to the community leadership or to their husbands. It asks simply that they keep quiet and remain subdued in the assembly of the community' (*MH*, 232). It would be bad enough if that were all the text said, but clearly it goes well beyond that. In these three examples from I Corinthians it is difficult to say which is the more surprising feature: the patriarchal tendencies of Paul, or Fiorenza's determination to deny their existence.

We can see in these chapters from I Corinthians that those who wished to find a religious legitimation for an ideology of domination would be well served in setting aside Jesus and the Gospels, in favour of Paul and his warmed-over Pentateuchal views. Nor do I think it possible to explain away these views or take comfort that they could have been worse. Fiorenza is right, however, to note that in many respects Paul is at odds with the life of the churches. It is therefore of considerable importance to examine a passage in Galatians in which Paul appears to change suddenly from addressing his readers as 'we' to addressing them as 'you', as if he were incorporating into his argument a baptismal formula widely used in the churches and quite independent of himself. It is likely that these words were addressed to those newly baptized:

. . . for in Christ Jesus you are all sons of God, through faith.
For as many of you as were baptized into Christ have put on Christ.
There is neither Jew nor Greek,
there is neither slave nor free,
there is neither male nor female;
for you are all one in Christ Jesus (Gal. 3, 26–28).

As we have seen, in the Gospels the distinctions and barriers which men create for themselves are made irrelevant to entry into the Jesus movement. They are neither conditions of entry, nor are they obstacles to entry. The specific categories mentioned might seem arbitrary to us today, but they covered the most obvious sources of division known to the ancient world. 'It was a rhetorical commonplace that Hellenistic man was grateful to the gods because he was fortunate enough to be born a human being, and not a beast, a Greek and not a barbarian, a free man and not a slave, a man and not a woman' (*MH*, 217). In the second century CE Rabbi Jehuda taught a prayer to be said daily:

> Blessed be God that he has not made me a Gentile.
> Blessed be God that he has not made me a woman.
> Blessed be God that he has not made me a boor (quoted *MH*, 217).

In Galatians 3, therefore, in discussing the relationship between the old faith and the new Paul is giving Judaism its place and putting it in its place. The old distinctions are irrelevant. This, of course, was good news and bad news. It was good news to those who had been oppressed, dominated and discriminated against in these various ways. It was good news especially to women who were no longer marginalized and humiliated. It was of course not so good news to those who had been privileged because of the chance circumstances of their birth. Men, especially men of power, authority and influence, objectively lost a great deal by entering such a community. Yet I do not think that Paul was here speculating about what should be. In his own practical way, I think he was observing the reality of life in these early communities, in which indeed the first were last and the last first. In Christ women and slaves could be leaders by virtue of the gifts of the Spirit. There is, however, something of more general, long-term interest in the categories which Paul includes in the passage, because among the three pairs here represented are all of the categories which I mentioned at the outset: race, religion, economics, politics and gender. All of these things exist, but now they are liberated from the previous uses to which they had been put by the ideology of domination. How different would have been the Christian church and how different its influence on Europe and the rest of the world, if Genesis 1 and Galatians 3 had prevailed! But the interests of domination were better served by Genesis 3 and I Corinthians. The Jesus movement was soon overtaken by the exotic and excessive extrapolations of misogynism.

Historically speaking, it must have seemed that with the emergence of the Jesus movement discrimination against women was at an end, at least wherever Christians met together. The old order of patriarchy, marginalization and inferiority was to be overtaken by a new egalitarian-ism of the spirit. The empire might not be transformed overnight, but at least the church would set a better example which might in time win over the evil world. Yet not only did the church fail to put such discrimination behind it, it reimposed patriarchy in a much more thoroughgoing way. Far from winning over the hearts and minds of an unjust order, the Fathers (*sic!*) of the church were far more misogynist than the pagans. A flavour of the new ethos is conveyed in a round up of some typical sentiments on the subject from the Fathers and those who influenced them.[6] 'A woman is as it were an infertile male,' claimed Aristotle, or alternatively, 'The female is as it were a deformed male.' Following this line Thomas described woman's nature as 'defective and misbegotten'. Philo of Alexandria claimed, 'The female sex is irrational and akin to bestial passions, fear, sorrow, pleasure and desire from which ensue incurable weaknesses and indescribable diseases.' Tertullian described women as 'the devil's gateway', while Clement of Alexandria, perhaps disclosing more than he knew, said, 'Every woman should blush at the thought of what she is.' Augustine taught that 'Sex is degrading to the soul', while John Chrysostom warned that 'Among all the wild beasts, there is none more harmful than woman.' Jerome drew the conclusion from Paul that 'it is bad to touch a woman'. But what would Freud have made of Leander of Seville, as in the course of training young nuns he describes the virgin's mystical communion with Christ as 'lying on the chaste couch with the bridegroom, while he encircles your head with his left hand and fondles you with his right'. The pathology and the paranoia continued and even intensified in the Middle Ages. By the beginning of the twelfth century Hilbert of Tours taught of the dangers to monks: 'Hurtful to holy men are women, avarice, ambition,' and a century later a Premonstratensian statute declared that 'the iniquity of women surpasses all iniquities which are in the world', and that 'there is no wrath greater than the wrath of a woman, that the poisons of vipers and dragons are healthier and less harmful for men than familiarity with women'.

But if these views represented the orthodoxy of the church, expressing the views of celibate theologians living for the most part removed from what might metaphorically be described as social intercourse, it was not the view of the ordinary people, who knew otherwise and knew better. A feminist reading of the history of Christian thought and piety, if it pays attention to popular faith, discovers a very different view of women present at the same time as these excessive and misogynist texts. A good example of this popular piety is to be found in the mediaeval cult of Mary, not the Blessed Virgin Mary, but Mary Magdalene. A detailed study of the legends and cult, from the eleventh to the sixteenth century, has been made by Elizabeth Moltmann-Wendel in a study which she shares with her husband, *Humanity in God*

(= *HG*).[7] (You will no doubt be familiar with the work of her husband Jürgen, dapper, brown-haired father of four daughters.) Mary Magdalene is one of the central characters in the Gospels. She had been healed by Jesus of a severe mental illness (Luke 8.2) and became one of his followers. During his ministry Mary is always given first place among the women followers of Jesus. Although the disciples fled, she was there to the end. God might have forsaken Jesus, but Mary did not. It was Mary who was the first to experience the resurrection of Jesus and to be given the commission to proclaim that he was risen. Since the resurrection is the beginning of Christian faith and the Christian church this ensures a quite unique place for Mary in Christian history. Her faith is unmediated by men, and she is portrayed as a responsible person in her own right, capable of initiative and insight. We know that there were women leaders in the early church, but the special place of Mary is confirmed not only in the Gospels, but even more remarkably in the non-canonical Gospels. There we read that she was a considerable preacher, surpassing the disciples – which with respect might not have been too difficult, judging by their performances in the canonical Gospels. We read that Peter even complains to Jesus: 'My Lord, we can no longer stand this woman. She takes away from us every opportunity to speak' (*HG*, 6). With the death of Jesus, Mary is represented as the one who inspires the dithering disciples and tells them what they must do. However, although the early Fathers of the church could acknowledge the primacy of Mary, calling her 'Apostle of all Apostles' the misogynist mentality sought to dispose of her. Augustine begins the process by which certain narratives in the Gospels are associated to her disadvantage. Luke's account of the anointing of Jesus says that the woman was a known sinner. John's account is quite different and places it in the home of Lazarus. His sister Mary anoints Jesus. When the two are run together Mary of Bethany becomes a known sinner and it is simply assumed that Mary of Bethany was Mary of Magdala. Thus the great leader of the early church, first witness to the resurrection, friend and lover of Jesus, is dismissed as just another sinful female, from whom nothing good can be expected. Yet if ordinary people could not believe this, popular piety was to rediscover her. 'Mary Magdalene won the hearts and heads of those in the mediæval feminist groups, and her charismatic personality, forgotten for centuries, like Sleeping Beauty, was awakened' (*HG*, 10). Legends of the eleventh century tell how Mary Magdalene was forced to leave Palestine, and travelled to France to the region of Provence, where eventually she was an active missionary in her own right, converting the pagan rulers of Marseilles, preaching and baptizing. Her cult grew through the mediaeval period and from the thirteenth century her apostolic work was depicted in stained glass. In the sixteenth century she was depicted as consecrating her brother Lazarus (*sic!*) Bishop of Marseilles. At the same time there has always been the suspicion that the greeting of Mary by Jesus at the resurrection, and her response, reflected a deeper relationship than merely teacher and disciple. At a time when Christianity at an official level saw sexual relations as dehumanizing and detracting from the spiritual life, in popular piety Mary is presented as a lively, beautiful, erotic woman. So, for example, she is the patroness of the mediaeval cosmetic industry (*HG*, 14). 'The beautiful Helen of Christianity skips along at the side of her lover, she rides in the hunt and becomes, when emancipated from the church, a picture of purest delight of the senses' (*HG*, 14). And Luther, reflecting on the relation of Jesus and Mary, declares that she 'loved him with a hearty, lusting, rutting love' (*HG*, 14). This composite mediaeval picture of Mary Magdalene does not reduce her to a great sinner, nor in presenting her as the lover of Jesus does it reduce her to a passive role. The sensuous, the erotic, the passion, the energy, the life which she exudes is also expressed in her prime place among the apostles of the church, as a healer, preacher, baptizer, one who welcomes sinners and assures them of God's grace. Christianity for too long has been impoverished by the exclusion of such a liberated and liberating person.

In a second parallel study, Wendel examines the mediaeval cult of Martha of Bethany. The image of Martha is that of the bustling housewife, who has no time to sit and listen to Jesus, in contrast to her sister Mary who sits there and gives no help with the arrangements for a meal. Men have rather smugly accepted that Mary got her priorities right, but woman have tended to identify with Martha, with the one who has to get on with the practical things without which nothing else can take place. They would like to have sat and listened to Jesus, joined in the discussion, perhaps enjoyed his company and shared in stories and laughter. But someone has to be out in the kitchen or when the meeting is over there will be no meal. The image of Martha is therefore of the woman who occupies the place of women, on the margin of important things. However we should note first of all that it is Martha – not Lazarus or Mary – who takes the initiative in inviting Jesus into the house, and it is she who calls her sister. There is an apostolic role here. But more importantly there is another incident involving Martha, recounted in John's Gospel, which culminates in the raising of Lazarus from the dead. In this narrative we see Martha in quite a different light. Jesus has been asked to come to Bethany, and as Mary sits (again) at home, Martha goes out to meet him. She challenges Jesus. Lazarus would not have died if Jesus had been there. Even so, she has faith that God will grant what Jesus asks. Yes, she believes in the resurrection, a general resurrection at the end of time. But more than that she confesses her faith in Jesus. 'Yes, Lord; I believe that you are the Christ, the Son of God, he who is coming into the world' (John 11.27). A confession of faith which Raymond Brown compares to that of Peter himself. Here is a woman of faith and insight, who shows initiative and approaches Jesus directly, not in a mediated or subordinate role. And it is this Martha who figures in the mediaeval cult. There she is depicted as a dragon conqueror. She herself appears sometimes as a nun, but often as a beautiful, elegant lady, a celebration of life. The dragon is a composite beast, being part snake, part beast and part lion. 'In mediaeval depictions, as in the Gospel, she has an active part in the victory over death – over the animal of the abyss. It is a picture of resurrection hope. Martha's activity is no longer defined according to her sex and thus devalued (as good housework) but is expanded to take on cosmic dimensions' (*HG*, 19). Legends of the twelfth century tell of Martha, Mary and Lazarus, forced to leave Palestine, travelling to the south of France, where Martha gains a reputation for her preaching. She is called on to deliver the people of the Avignon area from a man-eating dragon which lives in the River Rhone. She finds the dragon, and sprinkling holy water on it, subdues it and binds it with her girdle. Later she becomes director of a nunnery, and when a young man travelling to hear her preach is drowned in the river, she raises him from the dead. Many cultures have myths of a dragon which threatens the people and is killed by a warrior. Here, by contrast, the dragon is not killed but subdued by the woman Martha. Her weapons against it are not those of anger and destruction, but rather of purity and spiritual power. Wendel makes a feminist contrast here, of the snake/dragon, which represents the power of nature, of the goddess, which is perverted (and presumably could be redeemed). The male approach is to reject this power, to attempt to destroy it completely, exemplifying alienation from nature. The legend of Saint George represents the overcoming of the dragon and the victory of patriarchy. The Martha legend connects with traditions of the goddess and matriarchy. But above all Martha is here an independent woman, a co-worker with Christ in the spiritual overcoming of evil with good, who has been given power over death and is able to bring forth new life in a spiritual way in raising the dead. From the high point of her cult between 1200 and 1500 she has been repatriarchalized, till today she is 'the patroness of the cooks and housekeepers of Catholic clergy'! (*HG*, 33).

Wendel concludes that Christianity has therefore had two opposing tendencies in Western history. It has on the one hand exalted men and denigrated women, not only as individuals, but in the evaluation of characteristics which are taken to belong to the two sexes. But on the other hand this tradition has never entirely eliminated the religious expression of another experience of woman, and the valuing of female characteristics. 'It seems to me that prevailing elements of a matriarchal subculture have been ignored here, elements that reflect the Christian woman's own experience with freedom and that we women have failed to integrate. Although ignored, this subculture remains neither assimilated nor obliterated and is in many ways comparable to the spirituality of blacks' (*HG*, 49). She comes to this conclusion: 'Matriarchal modes of thought have preserved such basic human values as the self-reliant function of women; the integration of nature, the body, and sensuality; and the dream of a cosmic world of freedom. These are values that had been nearly obliterated by a patriarchal craving for domination' (*HG*, 50). We are indebted to Wendel for these studies. Religion was at the time clearly responsible for the domination of women and for the suffering directly associated with the pathological misrepresentation of women. It would have seemed logical if the ending of this situation was brought about by a rejection of religion. Yet the challenging of the ideology of domination was brought about from within religion, rescuing good religion from bad religion, saving religion for future generations. It was not simply that some men misrepresented women, not even that women accepted the false view, but that the vision of mankind as the image of God was made ineffective, and the early community described by Paul of those who were in Christ set aside. And yet we have to say that historically these myths and legends described by Wendel did not achieve the liberation of women or men. The inferiorization of women was a religious principle, and when in the Reformation the authority of Rome was challenged, this was to be one of the principles which was reinforced in the Counter-Reformation. The image of women was not a starting point for the Reformation, but in the long view the Reformation's greatest achievement might be the challenging and rejection of the mediaeval orthodoxy about women.

In this ecumenical age it has become fashionable to play down the disruption caused by the Reformation of the sixteenth century. Protestants are more inclined to accept certain relativities in the leaders of the continental Reformation, while Catholics can admit to distortions in the institutional life of the church at that time. It is very easy to overlook the fundamental issues involved. Sometimes these are better observed by outsiders. Marx made an interesting assessment when he claimed for Luther that 'he shattered faith in authority because he restored the authority of the faith'.[8] A friend of mine who is a Catholic priest in Liverpool said in some exasperation, 'We are all Protestants now.' This element of the Reformation has indeed permeated the churches and is one of the sources of tension between feminists and some of the main-line churches. Feminists are objecting, not to the authority of faith but rather to the arbitrariness of authority figures, particularly patriarchy, the setting up of a system of domination on the basis of the superiority of the male over the female. But the Reformation itself rejected the basis of this domination. Jane Dempsey Douglass expands on this issue in an article entitled 'Women and the Continental Reformation'.[9] She begins with Luther's rejection of the 'counsels of perfection', which were the basis of a two-tier system of holiness. Lay people were required to obey the law of God, but there was a higher standard to which only a few could aspire which included celibacy and virginity. If we look back to the analysis of Fiorenza, such requirements introduce conditions additional to those for entry into the Jesus movement or for baptism into Christ. For Luther there is a Christian calling, but the normal life of service to others is within marriage. The Reformers opened the Bible and found the exemplars of faith to be married men who made provision for their dependants, and married women who bore children, nurtured, cared for and guided them. God created man and woman to live together as one flesh. Indeed Luther understood this as a commandment to marry, rather than to be celibate. Relations between men and women were damaged by sin, but Luther did not see sex as itself evil or a source of sin. He assumed that Adam and Eve shared their sex life before the Fall. In the various Reformation confessions of faith there is a recurring theme, that the first purpose of marriage is that a man and woman should within it love and cherish each other. It is not seen primarily in terms of procreation or as a remedy for lust. Since marriage was regarded as the normal circumstance, the Reformers no longer regarded it as a sacrament, and it came within civil law. It seemed to Calvin very odd that those who regarded it as a sacrament should so vilify both marriage and women.

Those who are in Christ have the responsibility to witness to that faith and proclaim it to the world. It was therefore necessary for all Christians to have understanding of the faith. The movement which started with vernacular translations of the Bible and instruction in the biblical faith expanded to programmes of reading and writing and eventually to more general elements of counting and the basic science of the day. This elementary education was provided and was indeed compulsory, for all children, boys and girls. We see therefore that because of their reading of the Bible the Reformers rejected certain foundations of the mediaeval church and transformed the place of women. However, because of their obedience to the Bible, the Reformers also were guided by Paul on the status of men and women. Feminists will not be satisfied to know that Luther saw woman's place as the home, and her role as wife and mother. All the Reformers accepted Paul's teaching that women should be obedient to their husbands. And of course within the Reformed churches, although the clergy had a different relationship to the membership, the clergy were all male, even if most were married. Indeed there was an immediate loss of status in that the vocation to be a nun was rejected. We might say that women were therefore not as liberated as they at first were in the early Christian communities. Their situation was in some respects more like women within the Old Testament. And yet we must not lose sight of the fundamental change which had taken place at a theological level. At the outset I distinguished between discrimination against women which was conventional, culture-related and therefore subject to change in consequence of developments within society, and discrimination which is based on some moral or religious principle. The profound change which took place as a result of the Reformation was that although the Protestant churches were still characterized by patriarchy, this was conventional and culture correctible. The discrimination against women characteristic of the mediaeval Catholic church was a matter of religious principle. This meant that while in Protestant countries the place of women in the church could change as the status of women changed in society at large, this process could not take place in Catholic countries. We need not here trace the long, long process by which the place of women in Western societies has changed. This belongs in large part to the history of the feminist movement. The eventual outcome was that for example in Scotland the status of women in society at large changed to such an extent that there was no reason why women should not be ordained. The chauvinistic remarks of Paul were not regarded as theological reasons. Paul was after all reflecting the cultural situation of the early missionary church. The theological basis of an all-male clergy had been removed at the time of the Reformation. The ordination of women breached no religious principle. In the Catholic church it is still a matter of religious principle. The contrast between the two positions is highlighted in Scotland. In the same society in which women have the same status, regardless of which religious affiliation they may have, or whether they have any at all, it might be expected that they would be treated in the same way with regard to ordination. The Church of Scotland ordains duly qualified candidates without regard to gender. There are no conventional views of women which would prevent ordination. Indeed and more positively, it has been possible to initiate an entirely new form of ministry, a married couple, both ordained and working in the same parish. But although the Catholic church exists in the same society it does not ordain women. The change in the customary treatment of women or the conventional views about women are quite irrelevant to the matter, since the denial of ordination to women is based on a religious principle. It is not true to say, 'We are all Protestants now.' Catholic feminists might be Protestant, but the patriarchy is still Catholic. For the hierarchy as custodians of the Tridentine orthodoxy – none more so than John Paul II – it would be a complete betrayal of the faith if they were to agree to ordain women. Before women could be ordained in the Catholic church it would be necessary for the magisterium to redefine the Catholic view of women. Feminists might see this initially as a retreat from a false position adopted and developed from the second century.

I have not had time to discuss the work of Rosemary Radford Ruether, to my mind the most outstanding feminist theologian in the world today. A fine classical scholar with an established reputation in theology before she began to apply the feminist perspective, Ruether is continually breaking new ground, both in the issues which she raises and also in the responses which she is gradually developing. Many feminist theologians, especially in America, are Catholics, and they generalize the position of their church, as if all churches not only excluded women from the ministry, but had the traditional mediaeval attitude towards women. But in her book *Sexism and God-Talk* (= *SGT*) Ruether does ask this challenging question. 'Will the increasing participation of women in the ministry provide alternative options in the foreseeable future? Or has the recent entry of women into ministry in token numbers failed to challenge, for the most part, the patriarchal interpretation of Christianity?'[10] Or again she claims that 'Women win inclusion in this same ministry, without asking whether ministry itself needs to be redefined' (*SGT*, 200). However, I believe there is a world of difference between a ministry in which women work already and can through feminist perspectives lead the church forwards away from domination and a ministry from which women are still excluded altogether and to which they can make no contribution. Both churches exhibit patriarchy, but the one which is a conventional patriarchy has already willingly sown the seeds of its own destruction. The other patriarchy is based on a principle which must not be breached. The feminist contribution is significantly different in these two situations.

In 1978 I wrote of the feminist movement, 'it is potentially the most important development in human history . . .'[11] My views have not changed in this matter, but with the passing of the years I am disappointed that the emphasis is still on the word *potentially*. If I end this lecture with some critical comments, they should be seen as fraternal criticisms. They are certainly not intended to provide support for the detractors or comfort to the despisers of the movement. Nor do I wish to suggest that the responsibility for any loss of direction is due solely to feminists themselves. In any case, when the lines are drawn many men would want to call themselves feminists. We all have too much at stake here to allow the feminist movement to become the burden of a small proportion of women. And it is because there is so much at stake that it is necessary to criticize. Lack of criticism would be a sign of indifference. But let us not personalize and sloganize. For example, in any other critical discussion we find that those who hold a position under attack respond to the argument: 'My position escapes the force of your argument.' Too often feminists respond with the guilt-provoking words, 'I find your criticism deeply offensive.' We are criticizing positions and assumptions, not individuals. Nor will it serve the cause of feminism and the ending of domination to reject every criticism equally with the blanket charge that it is sexist.

At the end of our discussion I noted that ordination of women is not an issue for the Reformed churches. We accepted Ruether's comment that the presence of women in the ministry does not thereby transform that institution. Yet it does mean that the debate is now about ministry, not about women. The significance of this transformation can easily be underestimated. Since ordination is no longer an issue the status of ordination is changed. It is no longer the winner-take-all prize. As I have already indicated, those churches which ordain, regardless of gender, were able to adopt this position because of changes in society in general. The understanding of woman was no longer within the control of church leaders. It seems to me there is an instructive parallel between the issue of ordination in the Catholic church and the issue of contraception. When Paul VI issued the encyclical *Humanae Vitae* in July 1968 he wrote that he expected that it would arouse controversy. 'There is too much clamorous outcry against the voice of the Church, and this is intensified by modern means of communication.'[12] At that time I knew many Catholics who were making their own decisions in such matters 'We are all Protestants now', and were incensed by the teaching of the encyclical. They formed groups to discuss the issue and sought ways to publicise their rejection of the contents. News of such frenetic activity must have delighted the Holy Father. The encyclical had achieved its aim. To guide Catholics back to the method of natural rhythms? Hardly. At that time, on the assumption that no Catholic woman was using the contraceptive pill in Belgium, judging by sales within that country it was clear that all Protestant men, women and children were using it. No, the aim was to re-establish the authority of the magisterium. The Pope had run up a flag, a Catholic flag, and thousands who thought they were in control of their own lives saluted it. Birth control, which society at large regarded as a secular matter, as an a-moral issue, was by the encyclical restored to its position as a fundamentally religious issue. For a hierarchy which controls absolution, it is more important that people realize that what they are doing is wrong than that they immediately give it up. There is a parallel between the issue of contraception and the question of the ordination of women. Women are not pushing at an open door here, for there is no door at all. There is no question of women being ordained, given the understanding of women in the Catholic church. It is therefore the understanding of women which must be changed. Ordination cannot liberate women: the new understanding of women will lead automatically to ordination for those suitably qualified. And yet by making ordination the central issue, feminists reinforce the foundations of the very hierarchical and patriarchal order which discriminates against them. Once again it is not important that they wish women to be ordained; what is supremely important is that they have reaffirmed the Catholic view of the significance of ordination. Is the hierarchy threatened by the demand for the ordination of women? Of course not: as they sip a little wine after dinner, the (female) housekeeper having retired for the evening, they are in good heart. Only those who are essentially loyal Catholics – who have not become pragmatically Protestant – would make ordination the central issue. Give the church a bad name? Not a bit of it. Most opposition to the idea comes from Catholic women, and in any case every time an article appears on the Woman's Page of *The Guardian* it recalls more lapsed middle-class Catholics to their roots than ever did the well-intentioned Catholic Truth Society. Catholic feminists must be careful that in their choice of issues they do not reinforce the very ethos which denies them progress. I can say no more on the matter at this point, but its seriousness will become clearer when in chapter 3 I examine Leonardo Boff's criticism of the church.

There is a second critical question to be raised for the consideration of feminists in the struggle against domination through religion. Although some early works on women and religion were characterized by more verve than facts, contemporary studies are serious, scholarly and entirely worthy of the importance of their subject. The works to which I have previously referred were chosen for this very reason. There is an increasing volume of literature exhibiting a high level of historical, textual, and linguistic competence, treating issues in the religions of the Ancient Near East, the Hebrew and Christian scriptures, in patristics, and in the mediaeval and early modern periods. There are articles on the ancient Goddess Cult, the Earth Mother, studies in history of religions and anthropology of religion. There are books on witches in Europe and New England and articles on Quakers and Shakers as well as the Great Bliss Queen. Confronted by such an impressive accumulation of scholarship, what can we say, except – Why? Of course I am not asking for a justification of historical scholarship as such. Perhaps we should ask for such a justification from time to time, but in so far as feminist studies fall within the broad academic sphere of the humanities or social sciences, then historical studies in feminist subjects need no particular justification. The question 'Why?' arises because it would seem that for most feminist scholars, writing or rewriting history is not the sole or sufficient motive. There is the hope or intention to contribute to the liberation of women in the present day. My critical question therefore concerns not those who are only interested in feminist matters for purely historical reasons, but those who wish to use these studies in some way today. The motive seems admirable, yet it is seldom thought through, and for precisely this reason the potential of feminism may not be fulfilled. How can historical studies influence the situation today? It is simply assumed that they can. But what if they do not? Or worse, what if historical studies actually reinforce continuing structures of domination? To see how this could be so we must begin by noting the actual sequence of events. Those of us who believe that the domination of women by men is morally wrong have come to this judgment because of contemporary developments in our social consciousness. We have not learnt it from the past but experienced it in the present. This new consciousness enables us to reread and even rewrite history. The domination of women was present in history but was not considered an issue. It was taken for granted as part of the fabric of life. And so for those who wish to explore this subject there will never be an end to historical studies of all societies, all religions, in all periods. But does this contribute to the liberation of women? In my previous example, if we argue that women should have leadership roles in the churches, it is because we now know this to be just and fair, not to mention to the great advantage of the churches. But the determined pursuit of historical studies is in danger of reversing the order of the argument. Thus feminists have invested a great deal of time gathering evidence of female leadership in the early church. As I have already indicated, this would be interesting academic work considered as a contribution to our knowledge of historical sources. But the motivation is also to make use of this knowledge in the present day. And this is the danger. The argument somehow seems to suggest that because women had leadership roles in the early church, they should have them today. But we know they should have leadership roles, whether or not they had them in the early church. The approach has no force at all except as an *argumentum ad hominem* (literally), that it has relevance only to those who believe that the past should determine the present. But when that premise is granted, the feminist cause is lost. Historical probabilities and ambiguities concerning societies remote from us in time and place are certainly not going to provide the springboard for radical change.

There is a third criticism which might be made of feminist theology, indeed of feminists generally, a third danger into which they might fall, with the consequence that the movement would fail to achieve its potential. I have already raised the question of the supposed effect of historical studies. At best they provide detailed case studies of injustice. Men have institutionalized discrimination against women for their own advantage. This social evil can be documented again and again in historical studies. To what end? Is there not a certain naivety here? Did men do this through ignorance, so that with historical knowledge they will stop discriminating? In the history of the world, what system of discrimination has ever been brought to an end by exposing it as evil? It was said of one of the leaders of the French Revolution that he made the mistake of thinking that when he had spoken, he had acted. Women's liberation will not come about by piling up examples of male discrimination. We shall examine this theme further in the next chapter when dealing with the question of how black people have been urged to liberate themselves. The danger is that by putting the responsibility for ending domination on to men, women might reinforce one of the most fundamental elements in male domination of women, namely that women have been dependent upon men for their well-being. What is to be achieved by this ceaseless accumulation of historical examples of domination? Guilt? Are men to be made to feel guilty? And then presumably they will stop doing these things. They may feel guilt, and they will not stop doing these things, but it reinforces the role of women as carping and criticizing. Much feminist writing is, I regret to say, a theology of nagging. My regret stems from the fact that the remark will be misunderstood, and for many will be 'deeply offensive'. But let us not lose sight of the argument. The domination of women by men is wrong, but do feminists actually contribute to the ending of domination, or do they inadvertently contribute to its perpetuation? The 'mustiness' of feminist theology is understandable: Men must stop doing this; men must start doing that. However, although the foot-stamping and finger-wagging are entirely justified morally, they do not constitute a solution to the problem. The theology of nagging merely dignifies the age-old image of woman as scold by the addition of righteous anger.

Feminist studies have abundantly demonstrated that religion has been one of the most persistent and influential forces in the legitimation of the domination of women by men. Feminist studies have also provided examples where religion provided for the liberation of women. However, my fraternal criticisms all suggest that feminist studies on religion are not assisting feminism to fulfil its potential at this time. The reason is that exposing evil is not enough; challenging individual men or groups does not solve the problem. At this stage it will not be entirely clear why there is a problem or how it can be resolved. That will emerge only towards the end of chapter 3, but at that stage we have to conclude that feminist theology lacks a critical social theory which might enable it to develop beyond wrist-smacking and actually tackle the problem of the persistence of male domination.

two

The Power of the Black Jesus

There is an iron law of colonial history, that the colonial power defeats and attempts to discredit the first wave of leadership towards independence. By so doing the colonial power thereby guarantees support for the second wave, which is much more radical and dangerous. In retrospect the colonial power then looks back to the good old days when it was dealing with the moderates. It sees too late that during the first wave it shared many common values and assumptions with the moderates, which are rejected by the radicals. Although this iron law is exhibited best in Africa, it has also been repeated in America, where the position of blacks has been described as a case of 'internal colonialism'. The civil rights movement which began in 1954, and came to be identified in the minds of many people with the leadership of Dr Martin Luther King Jr, was bitterly opposed by powerful sections of the white community. It was attacked brutally in the streets, and less overtly in the aptly named White House. The powerful conscience was silenced by conscienceless power. The iron law came into operation, and the black community was forced into support of a second-wave leadership who entered the struggle with a demand for Black Power, now. The new wave did not subscribe to the old values of integration nor did it maintain the agreed basis that social and economic norms were to be set by the white community. And so far as the churches were concerned, they had now to deal with a leadership which denied that blacks and whites had a common religion. Dr King had appealed to white Christians to be true to the Lord they shared. The sermons of Albert Cleage were much more abrasive, as he addressed his Detroit congregation with these words: 'I would say to you, you are Christian, and the things you believe are the teachings of a black Messiah named Jesus, and the things you do are the will of a black God called Jehovah; and almost everything you have heard about Christianity is essentially a lie.'[1] The Black Power movement of the late 1960s deliberately set itself over against the values and assumptions of the main-line white culture, and yet white Christians were shocked to hear James Cone associate not only himself but the Christian religion with the movement. 'Christianity is not alien to Black Power; it is Black Power'.[2] The iron law of colonial history had been fulfilled once again. The oppressors, in refusing to deal with moderation, are responsible for the radicalizing of the oppressed. But it would be a mistake to think that only the demands of the oppressed are radicalized. Much more importantly, the people themselves are changed. The issue becomes the decolonization of the mind.

In chapter 1 I said that I could not take time to present in any detail the rise of feminist consciousness. Now I cannot take time to cover the rise of black consciousness, yet the positions represented by Cleage and Cone, for example, derive from black consciousness and not simply from a civil rights shopping list of concessions. I wish briefly to identify central features of this black consciousness. It arose not within America, nor even in Africa, but in the Caribbean. One of the most important elements is the concept of negritude, associated with Aimé Césaire, the Martinique-born poet. It was in his struggle against the cultural colonialism which exalted all things French and denigrated all things native that he came to affirm blackness. It was no longer a mark of disgrace. Nor was it in some liberal sense irrelevant. Blackness was to be positively affirmed. Nor can slaves be emancipated simply by their masters' decree. Slaves can only be freed of slave mentality when they themselves are responsible for making and declaring themselves free. Césaire saw the violence of this internal eruption as ultimately fruitful, like a volcano which destroys and then makes fertile. This theme of the therapeutic nature of violence is associated with the work of Franz Fanon, also from Martinique, a psychiatrist who, working in Algeria during the war for independence from France, took the part of the colonial people, and eventually was regarded as speaking for all colonials. Blacks in the Caribbean and in the Americas, North and South, he saw as a diaspora from Africa. Colonialism is in the mind of the subject peoples, and they can only be free by striking out, in this case against the white Europeans and Americans. They must recreate themselves, and certainly not model themselves on white society. American blacks, who were in some respects the most advanced, were at the same time the most disadvantaged. They thought they were free. We can see in this a criticism of the civil rights movement, which was based on asking whites for something. This slave mentality of asking was to be rejected in Black Power. A second danger for blacks in America was that in the civil rights movement they were asking to be treated like whites, to be allowed to enter white society. Fanon warned against this, and in so doing revived a powerful tradition which derives from two more Caribbean leaders.

The first was Edward Blyden, born in the Danish island of St Thomas in 1833. Out of love of Africa he emigrated to Liberia at the age of seventeen, consciously going back to Africa, the land of his ancestors. He advanced rapidly through higher education and by 1877 he was Liberian ambassador in London. He is one of the forerunners of pan-Africanism, the movement which conceived of the Negro race, dispersed throughout the world. He sought to make blacks everywhere conscious of their roots in Africa, to give them a consciousness of their identity and pride in the achievements of their race. One other theme from Blyden which was to be important in the 1960s was that although he himself was a Presbyterian minister, he considered that Christianity was not a suitable religion for blacks. It had deprived them of their history and their identity and seemed to be incorrigibly racist. He never became a Muslim, but he considered that Islam should be the religion of black people everywhere. Blyden therefore favoured separatism. Black people should not look to integration within America. Writing at a time when Europe was colonizing Africa, nevertheless Blyden called on black people to return to Africa, to their own land. That large-scale immigration did not take place, but Blyden was important in the formation of black consciousness, in creating in American blacks the confidence that they, too, had a land across the sea from which their forefathers had come, in which they had been proud and full of dignity and honour. These, too, are the themes of the fourth Caribbean leader we can mention, namely Marcus Garvey, born in Jamaica in 1887. Growing up without any education, he travelled and worked in several countries in the Caribbean and Central America, observing everywhere indifference to the plight of the exploited blacks, an indifference exhibited by whites but also by the middle-class blacks. In 1912 he went to London and made contact with the pan-African movement. Two years later he returned to Jamaica and set up UNIA (Universal Negro Improvement Association). His work was opposed by whites and by the black middle class. This was also to be a lesson learned by Black Power, that their constituency was in the poorest and most oppressed black communities. The middle-class blacks had almost made it into the white community. They were terrified of being treated as blacks. They had worked very hard to adopt the attitudes, values and life-styles of whites. Garvey was an admirer of Booker T. Washington, who also worked among the black urban poor, and when Garvey at last went to America, he was then opposed also by the integrationist blacks, notably by W. E. B. DuBois and other leaders of the NAACP (National Association for the Advancement of Coloured People). For Garvey blacks must be self-sufficient, for no one would ever give them justice, civil rights or economic security. And if they could not as a black minority be expected to challenge and change the whole country, Garvey looked to the decolonization of Africa as the first step. With the backing of Africa, it would be possible to challenge the American government and business community. Garvey managed thus to unite against him everyone with power and was eventually deported in 1927 as an undesirable alien. He left behind him a twofold message. Blacks should have no faith in integration. They should be sufficiently proud of their black race not to want to integrate with whites. He was strongly against miscegenation. Curiously in his separatism he expressed sentiments not unlike those of the Ku Klux Klan. The second message to black people was that they would not advance by invitation, but only by gaining power, power in America and a power base in Africa. In 1965 Dr Martin Luther King Jr stood at Garvey's monument in Kingston, Jamaica, and praised him for the sense of dignity and destiny which he had given to the black people. Yet Garvey's influence was to lead not to the first wave, to integration, but to the second wave, to Black Power. His separatism was to be taken up by the Black Muslims in their rejection of everything white, especially white religion. The question was whether blacks, now forced by the white comunity's intransigence into the arms of Black Power, would also reject Christianity. It is in this context that suddenly the work of Cone and Cleage appears in a positive and evangelical light.

When Black Power emerged in the late 1960s one of the leaders was Stokely Carmichael, who was born in Trinidad, though he later lived in New York and Washington. He had worked with SNICC (Student Non-violent Coordinating Committee) and after several years of harrassment and arrest for this work it was not surprising that he came to advocate Black Power and reject non-violence. Most of the themes which we have already noted are present in Carmichael's position – internal imperialism, institutional discrimination and indirect rule, rejection of assimilation. In the book which he wrote with Charles V. Hamilton, *Black Power* (= *BP*), he stresses the need for blacks to free themselves, to redefine their self-image. 'From now on we shall view ourselves as African-Americans and as black people who are in fact energetic, determined, intelligent, beautiful and peace-loving.'[3] They will not be led by the middle class who wish assimilation, nor will they necessarily aspire to the kind of values and life-styles of the white community. They will have to be self-sufficient and generate their own power to achieve their goals. Black Power therefore calls black people to a cause. 'It is a call for black people in this country to unite, to recognize their heritage, to build a sense of community. It is a call for black people to begin to define their own goals, to lead their own organizations and to support those organizations. It is a call to reject the racist institutions and values of this society. The concept of Black Power rests on a fundamental premise: Before a group can enter the open society, it must first close ranks' (*BP*, 58). He is speaking here of developing a consciousness and a life which is not simply permitted by whites, but is generated independently of whites and cares nothing about whether whites like it or not. This is indeed the negritude of which earlier leaders spoke. But oppressors do not let the oppressed go willingly. Carmichael had a long experience of what happens to those who ask for freedom. Whites have now taught him what he must do. 'Those of us who advocate Black Power are quite clear in our own minds that a "non-violent" approach to civil rights is an approach black people cannot afford and a luxury white people do not deserve. It is crystal clear to us – and it must become so with the white society – that there can be no social order without social justice. White people must be made to understand that they must stop messing with black people, or the blacks will fight back' (*BP*, 66). And fight back they did, with sections of the inner cities suffering riots on a scale never before seen. In these circumstances the white community self-righteously took the side of law and order, and for the most part the white churches went along with this. It had been possible to support the integrationist civil rights movement, for after all, it had attempted to make everyone white. But it was impossible to support Black Power when it led to lawlessness. Indeed by our iron law of colonial history we might say that Black Power of necessity had to break the law; it had to take up its position outside what the white community expected and would permit. The law said that blacks should be treated equally, and in this the whites had broken the law. This could only mean that blacks had to break the law, to assert and establish their own position. But surely the blacks went too far? They went beyond righteous anger and started looting shops and burning property just for the hell of it. Surely their leaders would condemn this? By no means. This was the violent self-assertion of which Fanon had spoken, the only therapy open to those who could not afford Blue Cross and Blue Shield.

It is in this context that James Cone began to write of the relationship between Christianity and Black Power. Viewed from the perspective of the white churches Cone's position was untenable and objectionable, a betrayal of the faith. But Cone was in double jeopardy. From humble origins he had progressed academically through some of the best academic institutions in America. He was now one of those middle-class blacks who was not to be trusted. He was by values and life-style largely acceptable to the white community and had most to lose by any assertion of the unity of the black people over against the whites. That was bad, but there was worse to follow, for he was by profession a theologian. Not a teacher of Islam, but of Christianity, that slave religion which had first taught their fathers as Carmichael said, to look to the heavens, while white men robbed them blind. That religion about which Blyden had warned them that it was inherently racist. That slave religion which had justified their humiliation and promised them compensation hereafter for all their sufferings. For the militant blacks religion was suspect, but Christianity was the white man's religion. Anyone holding to it might still be misguided, but anyone teaching it must be a Reverend Uncle Tom. And who could blame them? Had Christianity not done all of these things and more? It was time to leave all religion, or at least turn to Islam and the Black Muslims. Cone's task therefore was first of all to save Christianity, to save it from being identified with its own white racist past. He had to assert that this is not true Christianity. It is possible to be a Christian and not be led into an acceptance of racism. But Cone as a Christian wished to say more than this, and make a positive statement. Christianity was not identical with its previous racist forms. Indeed true Christianity, if properly understood, was concerned with precisely the issues of freedom and humanity which were central to Black Power. Cone makes this identification not simply as an apologetic ploy, but rather because he believes in both movements and must try to bring them together. As a rule of thumb we should therefore expect Black Power to set the agenda for Cone. He will then attempt to show how Christianity, properly understood, affirms in its own terms precisely these issues.

It is natural for us to take as of long term significance movements in which we are directly involved, but it must have been surprising for the white Christians to read in Cone's book *Black Theology and Black Power* (= *BT*) that 'Black Power is the most important development in American life in this century . . .' (*BT*, 1). More than surprising, it must have been scandalous for them to hear that Black Power 'is, rather, Christ's central message to twentieth-century America' (*BT*, 1). It is not a case of asking how an already existing theology is to interpret and evaluate the phenomenon of Black Power. To the contrary, according to Cone, Black Power is the way in which Christ passes judgment on America and the white churches of America. Recalling the riots and the looting this must have been altogether incredible and distasteful. Cone expects that this will indeed be the response. He must therefore provide a proper definition of the movement. The looting is only one aspect and it does not explain the underlying concerns. His understanding of Black Power runs very much along the lines already indicated, including freedom from oppression, from dependence on whites, the uniting of the black community. He does not advocate integration, but does not lapse into black racism. 'Black Power, then, is a humanizing force . . .' (*BT*, 7). And if it is a force for making the lives of blacks more human and humane, for freeing them from whatever binds them, then is it not also in the providence of God? Well of course it is not when viewed from the white perspective, or from a theology which is based on that perspective. What is required is a black theology, the theological perception of what is going on, based on the black experience. Nor is this 'ghetto theology' (*BT*, 32) to be simply a black middle-class interpretation of events. Black theology, based on the black experience, will actually contribute to the liberation of black people. Now while this might still be offensive and confusing to the white churches, it is an extraordinarily bold step for Cone to take. In the black community many assume that Christianity is incorrigibly white and will also be part of the means by which whites oppress blacks. Cone turns this around and takes the initiative. Properly understood, black theology will positively contribute to the objectives of Black Power, namely the humanizing and liberation of blacks.

We shall have to ask later whether Cone's work is actually theology, a black theology. Certainly to begin with it is a christology. Or rather it will be familiar to those acquainted with the Life-of-Jesus research, because Cone follows the example of many before him in associating the historical Jesus of the Gospels with his own central concerns. We might assume that there is some special significance in the choosing of the first sermon which Jesus preached. In Luke Jesus associates his mission and ministry with that of the prophet Isaiah. 'The Spirit of the Lord is upon me, because he has anointed me to preach good news to the poor. He has sent me to proclaim release to the captives, and recovering of sight to the blind, to set at liberty those who are oppressed, to proclaim the acceptable year of the Lord' (Luke 4.18–19; Isa. 61.1–2). These well-known words sweep through white congregations but make no impact. But what if they are heard by those who are poor and kept poor, those who are captive and cannot gain their freedom, those who through no fault of theirs are oppressed? What does it mean that Jesus comes to bring them good news? The prophet Isaiah meant these things quite literally and so apparently did Jesus. There is no indication that they are to be interpreted in some merely spiritual and non-material sense. Hence Cone's conclusion. If that is what Black Power seeks, and also what Jesus promises, then the two go together. 'Jesus' work is essentially one of liberation' (*BT*, 35). That is the programme as it were which Jesus sets out in his first sermon. It is not long before Luke tells us that these are the very marks of the mission and ministry of Jesus. When the Kingship of God comes near, what do we find? 'The blind receive their sight, the lame walk, lepers are cleansed, and the deaf hear, the dead are raised up, the poor have good news preached to them' (Luke 7.22). Cone points out that these are the people of the ghetto. God has taken their side. There is no doubt that Cone challenges the white churches to interpret the Bible more literally and stop avoiding the judgment of the text. However, we have previously noted that his agenda is set by the Black Power movement and its assumptions. We have noted that in the development of negritude one constant theme is that the oppressed must act to free themselves. The problem is that in the Bible so often it is God who acts and does things to people, for good or ill, blessing or judgment. Thus although in the two passages noted God shows his concern for the oppressed and Christ heals the sick, in neither case do the people free themselves. Thus the conclusion which Cone wishes to draw does not go well with the texts. 'Through Christ the poor man is offered freedom now to rebel against that which makes him other than human' (*BT*, 36). The legitimation of rebellion is what Black Power wishes to hear from Cone, but is Cone authorized and entitled to take this step? So runs the argument, if Black Power seeks the same goal of liberation as does God, then what Black Power does must be the hand of God. 'Black rebellion is a manifestation of God himself actively involved in the present-day affairs of men for the purpose of liberating a people' (*BT*, 38). Cone assumes that there is only one kind of freedom, and that freedom justifies its means. He draws Paul into the argument. 'For freedom Christ has set us free' (Gal. 5.1). Yet historically while Paul saw that Christ brought freedom from the curse of the law, it is less clear that Paul drew the consequence that all slaves must be freed. Cone flits back and forth between the existential and the political meanings of freedom. 'It would seem that Black Power and Christianity have this in common: the liberation of man' (*BT*, 39).

This problem is not peculiar to Cone, and should confront any theology of liberation which, for example, uses the Exodus as a paradigm. God frees the enslaved and the oppressed, and this by a violent act. But it was God's violence, not that of the slaves. Here again is the problem of human violence: does it achieve God's ends? We shall return to this point later when considering a criticism of Cone by another black theologian. The problem with taking the Exodus as a model is that it means that freedom becomes an empirical matter. If political freedom is not achieved, then no freedom is achieved. Yet we know of prisoners of conscience, including Nelson Mandela, who seem to be free even though in prison. And there is the historical example of Jesus himself, who is free to go to his death. Cone's problem is that if he does not identify Christian freedom with political, cultural and economic freedom then he will be accused of spreading the white opiate of the people around to calm the blacks down and reduce their expectations.

It is for this reason also that the commandment to love your neighbour and enemy is also problematic. The ethic of non-violence and love has been used against blacks by a white society which neither exhibited love nor eschewed violence as far as blacks were concerned. Small wonder that Cone sounds very much like Stokely Carmichael in his treatment of non-violence. He takes up the threefold matter of love, justice and power, as previously dealt with by Paul Tillich. Cone does not want a continuation of the old division in which blacks were to show love, while whites held the power and determined what was justice. 'Therefore the new black man refuses to speak of love without justice and power. Love without the power to guarantee justice in human relations is meaningless' (*BT*, 53). (Which sounds more like Niebuhr than Tillich.) This is one of the points at which the black theologians part company with the non-violent tradition both of Gandhi and of Martin Luther King Jr. It is the tradition of Marcus Garvey that justice must be guaranteed by power. Although Cone can speak about the power of love, it seems to mean no more than that black people who could make it on their own, choose instead to get involved in the struggle. But once that is said, there seems to be no power of love as distinct from simply the struggle for power. 'Love is not passive, but active. It is revolutionary in that it seeks to meet the needs of the neighbour amid crumbling structures of society. It is revolutionary because love may mean joining a violent rebellion' (*BT*, 113). This, of course, is the most contentious issue. So much of Black Power, as Cone outlines it, is perfectly reasonable and even admirable. But we wait in vain for him to say No to Black Power. No criticism appears and no limits are reached. He clearly does not wish to be used by white Christians who in condemning violence are seeking to maintain the system of violence from which as whites they benefit. But he does not want to be isolated either. It is not his struggle alone. He calls on the black church to take sides, for there are two sides. 'It cannot condemn the rioters. It must make an unqualified identification with the "looters" and "rioters", recognizing that this stance leads to condemnation by the state as law-breakers' (*BT*, 113). The refusal to be used is one thing, the 'unqualified identification' means that even black Christianity has no critical distance from this secular movement. The Black Power struggle then becomes the criterion for black theology. Nothing is allowed to criticize or contradict it. 'Black theology is not prepared to accept any doctrine of God, man, Christ, or Scripture which contradicts the black demand for freedom now ... All ideas which are opposed to the struggle for black self-determination or are irrelevant to it must be rejected as the work of the Antichrist' (*BT*, 120).

This is the danger. If black theology only repeats in religious terms what Black Power already says, then it seems superfluous. The real contribution of black theology to the liberation of blacks, and even whites, would seem to lie in a more dialectical relationship to the movement. In this it might even be said that the objective is to make Black Power more Christian, but this is the very opposite of Cone's programme. 'Black Theology seeks to make black religion a religion of Black Power' (*BT*, 130). Finally Cone falls into a Manichaeism of colour, so that black becomes good and white evil. 'Reconciliation makes us all black' (*BT*, 151). It can only be that Christ himself is black. In the modern world, 'Where there is black, there is oppression; but blacks can be assured that where there is blackness, there is Christ who has taken on blackness so that what is evil in men's eyes might become good. Therefore Christ is black because he is oppressed, and oppressed because he is black' (*BT*, 69).

There is something profoundly right in such statements and yet at the same time they are quite inadequate, even dangerously superficial. Cone has been much criticized since he wrote them, and has responded to some of his critics by developing his position over the years. In focussing attention on his early work I am not discounting these changes, but it is still true that his more 'balanced' work is less stimulating. This is not at all surprising, and I am sure that Cone would not object to being compared at this point to Karl Barth. Many of us who find Barth's *Church Dogmatics* unilluminating and wilful are nevertheless fascinated by his early writings. Barth himself came to modify his position, yet looking back would not retract, given the situation in which he first wrote. I quote some words from the *Church Dogmatics* in which Barth looks back to his early study of *Romans*, because they suggest a parallel with Cone's early contribution.

> Well roared lion! There is nothing absolutely false in these bold words. I still think that I was right ten times over against those who then passed judgment on them and resisted them. Those who can still hear what was said then, cannot but admit it was necessary to speak in this way. The sentences I then uttered were not hazardous (in the sense of precarious) on account of their content. They were hazardous because, to be legitimate exposition of the Bible, they needed others no less sharp and direct to compensate and therefore genuinely to substantiate their total claim. But these were lacking.[4]

What Cone wrote had to be said, if Christianity were to be saved from the misrepresentations prevalent in the white churches and foisted upon the black community. It had to be said if the misuse of religion as a weapon of racialism was to be exposed. And it had to be said if blacks were to have any thoughts that Christianity might even contribute to their liberation from racial domination. In such a context the words of Cone were profoundly right, and to reject or even modify them at that time would have been to silence their prophetic judgment on racism, and lend comfort to those who saw in religion a means of perpetuating domination. And yet it is in precisely this respect that they are inadequate. And lacking the other words which had to be said, not least to the black community, their promise of liberation was both superficial and for that reason dangerous. The criticism is therefore not of Cone, as if he had not moved on, but rather of a position which many still occupy.

We have noted that Cone's work is christology rather than theology, and indeed it may be less christology than an attempt to present a black Jesus who will legitimize Black Power. An even more dramatic example of this is to be found in the sermons of Rev Albert Cleage, minister of The Shrine of the Black Madonna, in Detroit. They were published in 1968 under the title *The Black Messiah* (= *BM*). If Cone is writing to defend Christianity in the context of Black Power, the added dimension for Cleage is the presence in Detroit of the Black Muslims, and their claim, after Edward Blyden, that Islam is the natural religion of the blacks. One of the problems faced by Edward Blyden in advocating Islam as the black religion was that even after Christians had stopped participating in the slave trade from Africa, Muslims continued to carry it on: although Christianity had an ambiguous past with regard to blacks, so did Islam. Cleage notes, therefore, that many blacks in America have rejected one religion but have not entered the other. In passing we might say that it is not a simple exercise to become involved in a completely different religion. It requires some kind of conversion. Cleage takes his lead, however, from Marcus Garvey. 'The only black leader in this country to meet this problem head-on was Marcus Garvey, who organized the African Orthodox Church, with a black hierarchy, including a Black God, a Black Jesus, a black Madonna, and black angels' (*BM*, 8). I take it that Cleage is saying that if blacks who traditionally have been involved in the Christian religion, cannot become involved in Islam, then they might still be drawn to a very different form of Christianity. If they have now come to believe that Christianity is the white man's religion, they might be attracted to another form of Christianity. The white man who has stolen their land, their history, their identity, has also stolen from the blacks their Jesus.

There is in Cleage's work a powerful mixture of ideology and religion, images and facts. As we have seen, colonialism begins in the mind: it is at the level of consciousness that the blacks must be freed – or rather, free themselves. Cleage is therefore concerned to break the identification of Christianity with the white community, and to break down the ethics, values and virtues traditionally associated with that religion. To achieve this he is willing to mix images and facts to make a powerful appeal to blacks. Clearly the most important issue for Cleage is race, the division of America into black and white. This is projected back into history. The ancient world is divided along the same lines. The nation of Israel was part of the 'black' world. The category 'black' here obviously has more than colour connotations. It has associations with those who are poor, colonized, coerced and oppressed, those who are identified by their race and despised because of it. In this context Cleage can make the following claim: 'Jesus was the non-white leader of a non-white people struggling for national liberation against the rule of a white nation, Rome' (*BM*, 3). It is a mixture of facts and images. The historical facts would not bear out this scenario, but it does create a powerful image. Jesus, who has always been portrayed to the blacks as an Anglo-Saxon, was apparently a foreigner. He was from the Middle East. If the world is divided into white and other, then he was definitely 'other'. It is not just colour – though let us be clear that this is a tremendously important psychological point to make when colour is a matter of disgrace and humiliation. When God was incarnate, he did not choose the white race, but the black. He did not associate with the rulers but the ruled. He did not take his place with those who have power to control and exploit, but with the poor and the oppressed. And it was to the poor and the oppressed that God made himself known. If Cleage is on historically weak grounds when he suggests that Jesus was leading a black nation in an armed rebellion, he is on very strong ground in denying Jesus to the white, powerful rulers of this world. The Black Muslims might reject Christianity as wrong, but Cleage opened up the possibility of choosing Jesus against the white community. This would be even more damaging than leaving Christianity behind, depriving the white churches of their exclusive control of the picture of Jesus. This appropriation of Christianity contributes to the liberation of black people. 'Our rediscovery of the Black Messiah is a part of our rediscovery of ourselves. We could not worship a Black Jesus until we had thrown off the shackles of self-hate' (*BM*, 7). Only in the context of negritude could blacks be attracted to a black Jesus. In the old slave religion, the white Jesus confirmed their inferiority, their shame, their guilt. But now they discover that God chose them. God chose the blacks. Just as Israel of old was the Chosen People, now the blacks are the Chosen People. What a transformation! What a revolution!

And this brings us to the contemporary situation. Cleage points to a revolution in America, blacks struggling to be free of their white oppressors. Now, where is the Black Church to stand? Is it to take the side of Christ – the white Christ of the white churches – or is it to take the side of the Black Messiah? The historical model is applied to the contemporary crisis. 'Jesus was a revolutionary black leader, a Zealot, seeking to lead a Black Nation to freedom, so the Black Church must carefully define the nature of the revolution' (*BM*, 4). I need not draw attention to the point about the Zealots, not in Manchester where Professor S. G. F. Brandon has contributed so much to this question, but we see here another mixture of fact and image. Whether or not Jesus was associated with the Zealots, he was still executed by the Romans. How is it that the white Jesus is always on the side of law and order, when the black Jesus was actually tortured to death by the white nation, Rome? Fact and image, but it is powerfully suggestive that in the race crisis in America, Jesus is on the side of the blacks: Black Messiah, Black Church, Black Revolution for the sake of the Black Nation. We can see how Cleage here very skilfully steals the high ground from the Black Muslims, otherwise known as the Nation of Islam. By the image of the Black Messiah, everything that is said about Jesus and the poor now belongs to the blacks. The enemies of Jesus are now the whites. And in the Old Testament context, by defining the Black Nation as the Chosen People, all the promises of God and the powerful images of prophetic religion now apply to the black community. The whites are Pharaoh to the black Moses. Cleage is not writing here as a historical critical scholar who takes the text to pieces and then goes out to lunch. He is above all a preacher, a conveyor of the Word of God addressed to the people, concerned with inspiring black people to lift up their hearts in troubled times. The chapters in the book are sermons, and each ends with prayer to God. 'Now we know that God is going to give us strength for our struggle. As black preachers we must tell our people that we are God's chosen people and that God is fighting with us as we fight. When we march, when we take it to the streets in open conflict, we must understand that in the stamping feet and the thunder of violence we can hear the voice of God. When the Black Church accepts its role in the Black Revolution, it is able to understand and interpret revolutionary Christianity, and the revolution becomes a part of our Christian faith' (*BM*, 6).

Within this context Cleage deals with various matters in a consistent way. He calls for separatism (*BM*, 14), so that black people can gather together and build the Nation. He can see this extending to co-operative buying, to caucuses of blacks in the professions, groups of mothers, of unemployed. They must organize their own world, which is not in the control of whites. On the pressing question of violence his line is similar to that of Cone. The violence is already there, legitimized by white law and order. Indeed whites were quite prepared to disregard the Constitution to preserve their illegal advantage. Love and peace and brotherhood will follow from justice (*BM*, 16–17). And of course in common with Cone we have the controversial claim: 'You ought to love the looters because they are part of the Black Nation' (*BM*, 18).

Within the religious sphere itself he makes some further points. Christianity is now the religion of the Black Nation, and not a matter of personal morality and individual responsibility. He associates the latter with the Christianity of Paul in contrast to the religion of the Kingdom preached by Jesus. Presumably because Paul was a Roman citizen he was white and began the whole process which in American history was so amenable to slave religion (*BM*, 43–4). This emphasis on the corporate nature of Christianity influences Cleage's view of baptism. To be baptized is to be introduced into the new life of the Black Nation, of which the church is the soul (*BM*, 32). 'This baptism is meaningful because you die to all your old Uncle Tom ways, the slave ways you used to have. And you are born again, you are resurrected in the newness of life into the Black Nation' (*BM*, 33). The same context is used to reinterpret the eucharist. 'But the broken bread is the symbol that we are willing as individuals to sacrifice ourselves for the Nation. The wine is the symbol that we're willing to shed our blood for the Nation' (*BM*, 33). Cleage can reinterpret the sacraments in this way because of his presentation of the intention and self-understanding of Jesus. He looks back to the Black Messiah who lived in a nation deeply divided against itself. 'He came to bring them together and to teach them that unity, love for each other, sacrifice, commitment and discipline were essential if they were to be free. His whole ministry was going about among a Black Nation preaching to them about the things that had to be done if they were to find freedom from oppression by a white nation, Rome' (*BM*, 24). Once again we are faced by the mixing of fact and image. It is virtually impossible now to reconstruct the self-consciousness of Jesus, and the many attempts end up by reproducing the consciousness of the writer rather than the consciousness of Jesus. So Cleage is not really describing first-century Palestine so much as the black community in America, deeply divided on the matter of violent revolution and relations with the white community. Thus Cleage sees many blacks acting like Judas, betraying their people. But then Jesus knew who they were, too, and was still prepared to go on with his vocation. For Cleage the death of Jesus is for the sake of the unity of the Nation, and he describes Jesus going up to Jerusalem with this one end in mind. Historically the facts are against Cleage, but once again he creates a powerful image of Jesus ignoring and rejecting the many ways by which people distinguish themselves from others and make themselves superior to them. He presents Jesus addressing himself to the poor and in consequence alienating himself from the powerful.

Finally, Cleage addresses himself to those who are not present in church, to the young militants who reject Christianity as the white man's religion. He adopts an approach originally illustrated at the very end of the eighteenth century by Schleiermacher. Schleiermacher addressed those members of the Romantic movement who considered that they had gone beyond religion. But what these cultured despisers of religion rejected was not true religion, but a distortion of religion, one which they were amply justified in rejecting. Was he dismayed that they rejected it? Far from it: he himself as a Romantic also rejected it, but for something better. So Cleage, himself a black militant, addresses the black despisers of religion. And if religion is the white man's religion then they are quite right to do so. But not right to assume that all religion is like this. There is a true form of religion, now presented by Cleage, which is very close to their own aspirations. He addresses himself specifically to Stokely Carmichael and other SNICC organizers and activists. If they come to his church they will never have to sing 'Fairest Lord Jesus . . .' But more than that. 'I address my remarks to those who believe in the Movement but who do not believe in the Christian Church because they do not understand that the Movement is the Christian Church in the twentieth century and that the Christian Church cannot truly be the church until it also becomes the Movement. So then I would say to you, you are Christian, and the things you believe are the teachings of a Black Messiah named Jesus, and the things you do are the will of a black God called Jehovah; and almot everything you have heard about Christianity is essentially a lie' (*BM*, 37).

Cleage did not expect whites to be attending his church to hear such sermons, and Cone begins his book by saying that he does not expect white people to hear what he is saying. There is also a danger that white people might view these two writers as dealing with matters internal to the black community. They might be fascinated by the sight of Cone trying to come to terms with Black Power, and Cleage trying to fend off the challenge of the Black Muslims. When we ask whether religion contributes to domination or liberation, the answer is in part whether white people are changed by the kind of material we have just reviewed. If the consciousness of white people is raised in any way, then we should conclude that religion has contributed to domination in the sphere of race, and has done so for centuries, but that from within the Christian tradition there is now a challenge to domination. Turning to the black community we should have to say that of course religion had been used for domination, but that the same religion, or at least a transformed understanding of it, could now contribute to the liberation of black people. There is, however, one major qualification. Does this black religion simply provide a religious legitimation for Black Power? We have seen that it would never occur to Cone or Cleage to criticize Black Power in matters of theory or practice. Everything that blacks do in this context is justified and explained. But is this religious legitimation the only contribution which Christianity can make to liberation from racial domination? We can pursue this possibility through looking at another black American, and then an African theologian and activist.

Coming as it did at the end of the 1960s, it was necessary for black theology to establish its relationship to other movements and theologies. J. Deotis Roberts, who wrote *A Black Political Theology* (= *BPT*), is one of the most impressive exponents of black theology, but he does not feel it necessary for a mature theology to attract attention by associating itself with high-profile media terms. Rather disarmingly he claims that American black theologians with few exceptions belong with the 'soft theologies of revolution'.[5] But in making his realistic statement, Roberts should not be thought of as a theologian retreating from the main issue. For him the issue is racism, the goal is its defeat, and as a theologian he has a contribution to make, especially through the black church. But he is right to emphasize that the new element in the situation is black consciousness. Black people will not be liberated if and when white people give them permission. The liberation has already begun. 'We have decolonized our minds . . .' (*BPT*, 22). Roberts is confident enough of his own position to be critical of those who conceive of black theology too narrowly. Just as the liberation of blacks must begin with blacks, and not with yet another cultural, emotional or psychological hand-out from whites, so black theology cannot be simply a mirror reflection of white theology. 'Black theology must not be a simple reaction to white oppression. It is rightly interested in the misinterpretations and the omissions of "white theology", which have often provided justification for the oppression of blacks, but it is considerably more than this' (*BPT*, 40). For whites who thought that with Black Power defeated, things could return to 'normal', Roberts comes with bad news. Black self-awareness is now quite independent of the white community. It is something positive in its own right. '"Black" is a symbol of self-affirmation' (*BPT*, 21). It is no longer meaningful only in relation to 'white'. Black theology therefore is not limited to the criticism of white oppression – though it will certainly pay considerable attention to it; it is a new theological perspective which arises from a positive experience. For those of us who have lived through this period of change one of the most astonishing features of the process, which could not have been predicted, has been the positive use of the term black – discussed earlier in connection with 'negritude'. Roberts as a theologian is quick to see the deeper typology in this acceptance. In the ancient world Christians saw how the cross, that weapon of cruelty and occasion of humiliation, was transformed in the providence of God into a symbol of comfort and of hope. 'There is even something Christlike in taking something shameful in the eyes of the white oppressor and investing it with pride and dignity' (*BPT*, 24). Racism continues, but in this transformation black people have already achieved their greatest victory: they are no longer dependent on the white definition of who they are or what they are worth.

It would be altogether unjustified to accuse Roberts of settling for freedom merely at some inner or private level. As we shall see, he goes on immediately to speak of political power and structural change, but without that *metanoia*, that conversion or transformation of self-understanding, outward changes would take place only within a continuing context of white supremacy. After all he is speaking of political theology, and when Johannes Metz defined it for the modern age he claimed that its primary critical task was 'the deprivatizing of theology'.[6] Roberts stands in this tradition and links it to his own situation. 'A privatized, quietistic version of theology is inadequate for the oppressed. What we need is a political theology – a theology of power' (*BPT*, 26). He does not avoid the issue of power, but he refuses to come at it in the terms offered by the confrontation of Black Power and white power. In this Roberts emphasises that he is attempting to do theology. He is very critical of Cone and Cleage, both of whom he considers to be more closely – and uncritically – aligned to Black Power. Both tend to reduce theology to christology, and indeed reduce christology to the dangerously superficial question, 'What would a black Jesus be doing today?' Apart from all the problematic assumptions embedded in this question, it has lost its theological dimensions. By contrast Roberts insists, 'We have the need for more than a moral example in Jesus. We need a saviour as well. Not the Lamb of God who pays it all and saves us one by one. We understand him to be one who is able to work *in* and *through* us to will and do beyond all that we are able to ask or think on our own' (*BPT*, 125). In this way Roberts brings to

political action enabling grace rather than religious legitimation. He has
criticized an understanding of grace which performs a metaphysical
transaction, but leaves relationships within the world unchanged and
political structures unchallenged. Roberts pursues the same dialectic in
turning to the familiar question of the relationship of love and justice.
He is quite clear that there must be actual change, that liberation must
have also objective political and social gains. The rewards of religion
have been too long preached to black people as referring to the next
world. 'We have had "heaven" – now we want some of this earth' (*BPT*,
41). Indeed this is one reason for the disenchantment of impatient
young blacks with the church. 'We have had our fill of pearly gates,
golden streets, and long white robes. We have sung songs about heaven
until we are hoarse, but our poverty and misery have gone unabated'
(*BPT*, 180–1). Roberts has considerable sympathy for the work of Dr
Martin Luther King Jr and the Southern Christian Leadership
Conference, but at the end of the day has to agree with the assessment
by the National Committee of Black Churchmen that the 'powerless
conscience' did not overcome 'conscienceless power'. It was because of
the intransigence of whites, all the way to the White (sic!) House, that it
was necessary to raise the issue of Black Power. But Roberts does not
simply join that camp. His constituency is the church, 'the slumbering
giant' in the black community. Perhaps Nietzsche was correct in
claiming that Christian ethics have made people reluctant to seek and
use power. Roberts is not speaking of the power of the gun when he calls
for a moral and theological use of power. 'A black political theology is
designed to awaken this most powerful black institution in the cause of
the liberation of the whole man' (*BPT*, 69–70). By this last phrase he
means what Asian theologians have called 'integral liberation',[7] a
liberation which is inner and spiritual, but not privatized, which is outer
and structural, but not materialist. By developing this more subtle and
sophisticated understanding of the objectives of black theology, Roberts
is then able to relate it to Black Power. In his case Black Power is
understood in a theological context: for others theology is in danger of
being subsumed under Black Power. Instead of being the title of an
abrasive movement, he tends to use it as a suggestive concept. He even
draws a parallel with the term 'conscientization' as used by Latin
American theologians. The phrase 'black power' he claims has the same
function for North Americans. 'Black power symbolizes a number of
images and ideas drawn from black history and the black experience:
black consciousness, pride, self-respect, community control, repara-

tions, empowerment, personhood, and peoplehood' (*BPT*, 170). The spectrum here is also 'integral'.

Having established the meaning of black power, and its relationship to black theology, Roberts must still face the fundamental issue, real change. Quite apart from, or rather in addition to, any inner transformation, there must be structural emancipation. The oppressed must go free, which means in practice that the oppressive system must become a liberating one. And since this is theology and not humanism, this must mean that it happens because God acts today as he has done in history. 'A black political theology sees God as a God of love and justice whose power is sufficient to oppose every structure that denies the humanity of the black poor and all the oppressed among humankind' (*BPT*, 116). And this is the problem. Quite apart from what must be the case, what if such liberation does not come about? What would this mean for the doctrine of God? Has Roberts succumbed at this point to the rhetoric of Cone and others who use the Exodus as a model for liberation? The problem is not unique to Roberts, indeed it is not peculiar to black theology. It is common to all theologies of liberation. Perhaps it is or should be a problem to all theologians. How does God deal with his people? Is the answer Exodus or is it Diaspora? Does he gather them out of the nations, or does he disperse them into the nations? Or is it both? Or should we not rather say that at least for Christians, there is no typology of God's actions apart from Christ? The divine creativity is always offensive and unpredictable. To insist that the liberation of a particular people in specific socio-political circumstances will take place by the hand of God is always disastrous. Inevitably the prediction is proved wrong, if only because God does not repeat Exodus again and again. It is also disastrous because the claim seems to draw up an empirical test of either the nature of God or the existence of God. For all his avoidance of the reductionism of a too close association with Black Power, Roberts comes close promising what God may decide not to deliver. But as I have already indicated, the problem of appealing to Exodus, to the oppressed going free, is a problem for all theologians. Briefly, the problem arises not from the possibility that the Exodus did not happen as reported, but rather from the possibility that it did. The problem is not convincing the doubter that God sent a plague to kill innocent children, but rather believing that the God and Father of Jesus Christ would act in such a way. No black theologian would be willing to accept the liberation of his people at such a cost, and if he did would he not have forfeited that justifiable and striking claim made by Roberts at the outset about the Christlike experience of the newly emancipated black community? This is indeed the bottom line for black theologians: if they are not to be jeered at as Rev Uncle Toms, how is the liberation of which they speak more than the old inner peace and pearly gates? He has to find a course between the ethics of Black Power activism and the eschatology of future rewards. 'We need a bringing together of ethics with eschatology in a way that will empower blacks for a better life now. To this end Christians must become collaborators with God and each other. We must then begin to spell out what are the theological perspectives on a new self-image, social solidarity, self-determination, community control and empowerment programs as well as the message and mission of the black church in the cause of black liberation. Only in this sense may ethics and eschatology be brought together in black theology' (*BPT*, 182–3). This is in the right direction, though it falls short of being a specific answer to the problem. Roberts is quite clear that black theology can provide a practical alternative to the more frenetic Black Power. Its task is to show 'how the Christian faith may implement black power here and now in constructive programs for the liberation of the oppressed' (*BPT*, 182). Although Roberts returns again and again to the black church as his base, he would have to indicate how the church might change and develop to become the instrument of this liberation, especially if the way advocated by Dr Martin Luther King Jr is not accepted as adequate.

If there is an answer to this question, then it lies in the experience peculiar to the black church. Just as black theologians now see the extent to which the theology they were taught was actually white theology, so it is possible to see the form of the Christian religion practised in the black church as reflecting white religion in terms of spirit, ethos, ritual, architecture, liturgy and government. Nevertheless even within this given form the black church has developed characteristics of its own. As the characteristic features of the white churches can be traced back to their European past, so now black Christians are tracing the characteristics of their religious experience back to Africa. This can be seen as a further step in the decolonization of the mind. The concept of blackness has been transformed from negative to positive. Similarly Africa, until recently regarded even among blacks with disdain, is now regarded with great affection. In the liberation of black people the idea of Africa has been immensely important as a counter to the white roots in Europe. Roberts refers to Presbyterians who still look with great affection towards Scotland. Perhaps they never visit it, and perhaps this is no bad thing if they wish to preserve an image rather than discover a reality. Similarly it is the idea of Africa rather than the reality which is important. 'Most blacks do not need a *real* home in Africa; they need a *symbolic* home there' (*BPT*, 53). Roberts thinks that black Americans might be a bridge between the USA and the Third World. This is an interesting suggestion, but it could only be based on closing any possible gap between the real home and the symbolic home, in the sense that black Americans would have to come to terms with Africa as it is in reality and not in some selective fantasy. In the film, 'Little Big-man' the old Indian chief recalls a negro by referring to the 'black white-man'. Viewed from outwith the USA blacks still appear to the rest of the world as Americans. This is nowhere more evident than among American blacks who visit African countries. Roberts claims that 'Black religious experience is Afro-American. We are in essence a people whose religious roots are in the villages and forests of Africa' (*BPT*, 55). But that romantic view does not provide the basis for a bridge to the Third World. Links with the Third World exist, but they are contemporary, not historical. For example when Roberts turns to the question of theodicy – the problem of reconciling human suffering with the justice of God – he is very close to some of the Latin American theologians. As we shall see, in Latin America the problem of suffering is not regarded as a philosophical but as an ethical matter. There is a close parallel when Roberts contrasts the attitudes of whites and blacks on the issue. 'The privileged need definitions, rationalizations, logical conviction, and language clarity to understand liberation, justice, and mercy. The oppressed have an immediate and intuitive understanding of such things' (*BPT*, 38). It is here that blacks come close to being a bridge to the Third World, not in some romantic musings about historical sources which play very little part in the determination of their consciousness today. Another example concerns theological method. The matter has been much more fully explored in Latin America, and we shall examine it later in that context, but it is a characteristic of many Third World theologians that they begin from the actual situations in which people live, rather than a metaphysical picture which is supposed to describe how they live. If Roberts developed his theology along these lines then this would be another link with the contemporary Third World. Black theology, he tells us, 'is not primarily involved in a repetition of its creeds and dogmas. The situation of man in the world is normative for political theology, of which black theology is an expression. Political theology brings an essential corrective to existential theology because it perceives

existence no longer as purely spiritual, but as sociopolitically condi-
tioned. This approach to theology involves the merger of theory and
praxis' (*BPT*, 190).

This final phrase, however, raises a fundamental question which
black theology has yet to answer. From what do blacks require to be
liberated? Or to put it another way: What are the impediments against
which blacks have to struggle? Roberts has noted that some black
theologians, like many Latin American theologians, do their work in the
context of the poor and the oppressed. But, he concludes, 'Ours is more
of a race problem than a class problem' (*BPT*, 207). This may be the
weakest feature of black theology, the greatest obstacle to its further
development. It is the analysis of a black white-man and places black
theology firmly within the American context. At the same time it opens
up again an immense gap between black theology and that of the Third
World.

Roberts is in agreement with Cone and Cleage that religion has in the
past been used as a weapon against black people and has legitimized
discrimination by whites. But when we turn to the possibility that this
situation might be brought to an end and that religion might actually
contribute to the liberation of blacks, then there is a marked difference
in his position from that of the other two. Christianity cannot be simply
remoulded in terms of Black Power, nor can we assert an identity
between the self-consciousness of Jesus and the objectives of that
movement. Roberts is careful to pursue theology and not simply a
Jesuology. But is it even that? Can there be a Christian theology today
which elevates the experience or problem of one group to provide the
criterion of theology, especially if that group is itself poised between
being oppressed and causing oppression, between suffering and
benefitting from the suffering of others?

We noted that any criticism of feminist theology is often repulsed by a
charge of sexism. It would be very easy to reject any criticism of black
theology with a charge of racism. For this reason the most illuminating
evaluation of black theology in America comes not from American white
theology, nor the theology of Europe, but from that great homeland
across the sea, from Africa itself. The possibility of a direct comparison
between American black theology and African black theology lies in the
coincidence that Allan Boesak has written a book entitled *Black
Theology/Black Power* (= *BT/BP*).[8] While black theologians in South
Africa have been initially indebted to their brothers in America, the
fundamental difference between the two perspectives soon emerges. It

is significant that Boesak at the outset explains that he is dealing with 'the meaning of blackness in South Africa' (*BT/BP*, xi) in dialogue with North America, but also Latin America, Asia and the rest of Africa. It is strange that in all the talk about Africa in American black theology, it is Africa as an idea which is important, and not the contemporary experience of Africans.

Boesak's book has also been published under the title *Farewell to Innocence*. The innocence of which he speaks is in fact a pseudo-innocence, perhaps even what Sartre calls 'bad faith'. It is the attitude of the oppressed who because they are given no responsibility eventually think of themselves as being incapable of responsibility. Boesak reflects the American experience. 'Getting rid of an implanted slave mentality is central to the philosophy of Black Consciousness' (*BT/BP*, 6). It might seem that Boesak is simply going to borrow from American black theology – which would be an interesting case of cultural neo-colonialism within the black race. But Boesak makes an important distinction. It is necessary for black consciousness to be raised and black people to examine their experience, but Boesak is writing theology, and the source of theology does not lie within the experience of a particular group. Yes, theology also has to be reconstructed and liberated from previous abuses, but it cannot be identified with the black experience.

Cone, we have noted, speaks of reflection 'in the light of the black situation'. This formulation calls for caution. The black situation is the situation within which reflection and action take place, but it is the Word of God which illuminates the reflection and guides the action. We fear that Cone attaches too much theological import to the black experience and the black situation as if these realities *within themselves* have revelational value on a par with Scripture. God, it seems to us, reveals himself *in* the situation. The black experience provides the framework within which blacks understand the revelation of God in Jesus Christ. No more, no less (*BT/BP*, 12).

Black consciousness can assist in the liberation of theology from distortion and the reading of the scriptures from misinterpretation, but the black experience is not the norm or criterion for theology. This is a fundamental point, and addresses itself to our previous question, whether Cone sells liberation short by merely legitimizing Black Power instead of adding new possibilities raised through a new non-racist Christian perspective. I believe Boesak detects in Cone's work a kind of American parochialism. If in the South African situation he were to restrict theology similarly to 'indigenization' it would serve apartheid very well by becoming simply a 'homeland theology' (*BT/BP*, 14).

Part of Boesak's suspicion of Cone's position arises from his view of the nature of Black Power itself. In this he tends to follow the lead of Martin Luther King Jr who maintained that Black Power was a revolution born in despair and without hope, a revolution doomed to fail (*BT/BP*, 60). The place which Black Power gave to violence ensured that it only imitated white society. As King said, 'In advocating violence it is imitating the worst, the most brutal, and the most uncivilized value in American life' (quoted *BP/BT*, 61). This is a complex and central issue and there is an impression that Boesak, like King before him, is struggling with the issue not only as a question of strategy, but as a fundamental issue for a religion whose founder died on the cross. Blacks in America were not facing a more violent régime than blacks in South Africa, yet Boesak is searching for something more profound than tactics. He quotes King with approval. 'Humanity is waiting for something other than blind imitation of the past, if we want truly to advance a step further, if we want to turn over a new leaf, and really set a new man afoot, we must begin to turn mankind away from the long and desolate night of violence' (quoted *BT/BP*, 70). Those who criticized King, Boesak considers, share the very ideology of the powerful who rule and oppress.

Boesak is suggesting that Cone's theology has no religious depth to it, it adds nothing to the ideology of Black Power. It is one thing for the Black Power movement within America to be concerned with this one issue and this one situation, but if Christianity is to be a universal religion, then the agenda of Black Power cannot be the limits or the criterion of theology. Boesak therefore offers a further criticism of Cone. 'Cone's mistake is that he has taken Black Theology out of the framework of the theology of liberation, thereby making his own situation (being black in America) and his own movement (liberation from white racism) the ultimate criterion for all theology' (*BT/BP*, 143). Boesak is pointing once again to the parochialism of Black Theology in America. The black experience is not the criterion for theologians in Latin America, certainly not the experience of black Americans. The frame must be turned round the other way. Black theology must be seen as one mode of the theology of liberation, not its only or ultimate expression. Incidentally Boesak is prepared to criticize Roberts, though he appreciates that Roberts distances himself from Cone. But on this point Roberts is no different from Cone: neither offers any fundamental criticism of American society except that the American pie is not being sliced equitably (*BT/BP*, 133).

Not surprisingly Boesak is critical of Cleage. He sees that Cleage too uncritically identifies Christianity with Black Power, subsuming religion under ideology. What we have called parochialism also appears, since God's chosen people are envisaged as black Americans. It never seems to occur to Cleage that black Americans might be oppressing other non-white nations. But beyond these matters there is something of particular concern to Boesak, living in South Africa. Separatism in Garvey was not dissimilar to the goal of the Ku Klux Klan. Separate development as advocated by some Black Muslims can be used to justify apartheid in South Africa. Boesak sees the same separatism in Cleage. Roberts stresses liberation and reconciliation, but the latter is omitted in Cleage. In passing we might note a further point which Boesak does not mention, but which is relevant. The stress on the Nation, on race, on the homeland which is found from Blyden, through Garvey, to the Black Muslims and Cleage, is reminiscent of fascism. Indeed although fascism is a notoriously difficult concept to define in political theory, these elements recur in any of its forms. The founders of apartheid in South Africa were sympathetic to German fascism. There is something odd about a movement for liberation which keeps such company.

So far we have examined the place of religion in domination and liberation in the context of gender and race. We have still to consider economic class, but already a pattern is emerging. Although it is possible to see how religion can contribute to domination when these fields are taken separately, it would seem that religion, or at least the Christian religion, cannot assist in liberation when only one level of discrimination is tackled. Paradoxically, by concentrating on one, those who seek to end that which oppresses them only succeed in ensuring that that which oppresses others continues. Thus in these early examples of black theology we find no sensitivity to the fact that black men oppress black women and would continue to do so even if the objectives of Black Power were achieved. Or again, many feminists seem quite unaware of the fact that their social and economic class is the source of the most acute oppression of other women. Further, as an American feminist admits, 'While few, if any, of us white women intended to exclude the lives of women of colour from our concerns, we simply had not begun to comprehend the extent to which women of different racial/ethnic groups have disparate historical and contemporary experiences of sexism.'[9] Through cultural imperialism for example, American women generalized about 'women's experience'. Their aspirations were not necessarily the aspirations of Muslim women, or women from Sri Lanka.

Another aspect of the emerging pattern concerns what in the last chapter I called a lack of critical theory. Then I asked how feminist theology could contribute to liberation when it had no explanation for the fact that sexism is more than an accumulation of the attitudes and actions of individual males. Similarly, black theology seems to have no interest in explaining the phenomenon of racism. But a condemnation of particular examples of racism is quite ineffective. After the civil rights movement beginning in 1954, and after the Supreme Court ruling of 1964, racism continues. Is this not puzzling, to say the least? But can black theology contribute to liberation if it has not understood racism? Not understanding racism is, of course, quite different from daily experiencing racism. The lack of critical theory throws black theology back into the ineffectual romantic repetition of rhetoric, the suggestive but inapplicable models and paradigms of the Bible. Roberts, who has certainly gone beyond Cone and Cleage, cannot make the breakthrough.

Finally, when we turn to Allan Boesak we encounter a complex and convoluted process. While it is true that Boesak begins with the familiar assertions of American black theology, eventually we are forced to the conclusion that Boesak is not writing black theology at all. Of course in his immediate situation he can apply the perspective of negritude to the internal situation in South Africa, but he immediately moves on from there. Whether consciously or intuitively, I believe that Boesak knows that to take the view that the only issue in South Africa is race would be to agree with the architects of apartheid at a fundamental level. Race is neither a moral nor a religious issue, but justice is. When Boesak writes – and acts – on race he does so because of his concern for justice. It is not trite to say that when he speaks of injustice, he does so out of the black experience, but when he speaks about justice, he does so as a Christian. It is for this reason that, as he says, the black experience is not the criterion of his religion. It may well be that what has been said here about Boesak was true about Dr Martin Luther King Jr, who was motivated by love and not by demands for equality of opportunity to fight for a large piece of the American pie. It is no coincidence that Boesak is influenced by King, who was influenced by Gandhi, who first began his work for justice in South Africa before returning to India.

If Boesak began by assuming he belonged with the black theologians, he soon found that he had little in common with black American theologians. More significant than their common colour was the deep division of their experience. Black Americans as Americans belong to the First World, and Boesak belongs to the Third. And as we have seen, it is questionable whether feminist theology or black theology, which belong to the First World, actually liberate, though they sometimes call themselves 'liberation' theologies. To see whether theology can actually contribute to liberation we must turn now to our third area, domination by economic class.

three

Marx and Liberation Theology

The Great Fire of London, the Great War: the title is bestowed properly not on events of which we approve, but on those before which we are overawed. So much destruction that things can never be the same again. The most significant casualty of World War I was the European world-view, which included assumptions about the rightness of social relations. These assumptions died in France along with the 'lions led by donkeys'. The corresponding casualties of World War II were the assumptions about the essential rightness of world relations. Europe had demonstrated that it was not morally equipped to lead the world, but in the post-war years it lost the will to exercise colonial rule. In the 1950s and 1960s decolonization movements pressed against doors which if not open were at least guarded without great conviction. As the old world consolidated its division into NATO and the Warsaw Pact, newly independent countries constituted a Third World, unwilling to be subsumed under one or other form of neo-colonialism. It is ironic that one of the most important factors in assisting the Third World to distinguish itself from the European-based conflict has been Marxism, a philosophy produced by the European Enlightenment, the European industrial revolution and, above all, the European form of the Christian religion.

The title of this book *Domination or Liberation*, is itself an indication of the extent to which the philosophy of Marx has permeated modern critical thinking, especially in the area of social relationships. Yet the influence of Marx is very recent. We have not long since passed the centenary of his death, and yet his writings have been important only in the last thirty years. Given his objective importance today, it is almost incredible to recall that his copious writings were out of print and not available for most of this century. Their publication came to be controlled in Moscow, after the Revolution of 1917, and the collected works were published in Russian. Little was known of Marx's philosophy thereafter and it must be said that there was little interest in the works of a man who came to be associated first with Leninism and then with Stalinism. The European communist movement, with its roots in the nineteenth century, was therefore increasingly drawn into identifying with and supporting the actual policies of the USSR. Not surprisingly the crisis came to a head after the death of Stalin in 1953, when his successor Nikita Khrushchev, at the famous Twentieth Party Congress, revealed and condemned at least some of the excesses of the Stanlinist years. This led to pressure for liberalization in the Eastern bloc countries, and subsequently to the invasion of Hungary in 1956 by the USSR to put down this movement. Fortunately for European communists in that very year publication began at last in Berlin of the *Marx-Engels Werke*. The writings, as they began to appear, presented a philosophy substantially different from what had been assumed to be Marx's position. Indeed the early writings, the works of the young Marx, seemed to be in important respects critical of the kind of régime present in the USSR under Stalin, and even under Khrushchev. The invasion of Hungary marked the parting of the ways, but the appearance of the philosophy of the young Marx made possible an alternative. By 1957 there appeared in Europe what came to be called the New Left, and it was possible for the first time to make the important distinction between being communist (Moscow orientated) and Marxist (being in general agreement with Marx's own philosophy). It was even possible to mount a Marxist critique of communism: indeed in this Marx had himself led the way. By the mid-1960s the writings of the young Marx swept through the universities of western Europe with their exciting criticism of institutions of manipulation and privilege, providing a new generation with a radical idealism which called for social justice, and an end to whatever dehumanized men and women in modern industrial society.

Earlier I said that it was ironic that neo-Marxism should have been more influential on the Third World countries than on those of the so-called First and Second Worlds. After all, the philosophy of the young Marx arose from a very particular matrix of circumstances in nineteenth-century Europe. The critical philosophy was an appropriation of the work of Hegel and could only be properly understood as post-Hegelian and certainly not as a rejection of the master. Marx dissociated himself with those who thought it fashionable to denigrate the System. Ten years before his death the mature Marx still sees his debt to Hegel. 'I therefore openly avowed myself a pupil of that mighty thinker, and even, here and there in the chapter on the theory of value, coqueted with the mode of expression peculiar to him. The mystification which the dialectic suffers in Hegel's hands by no means prevents him from being the first to present its general forms of motion in a comprehensive and conscious manner.'[1] It might be thought that there could have been nothing more calculated to make Marx inaccessible to the Third World than his 'coqueting' with the great dialectical metaphysician of the nineteenth century. But even when Marx turned to more practical matters, he did not seem to move towards the situation of the Third World. For example, he was much influenced by the Scottish political economist Adam Smith and his analysis of *The Wealth of Nations*. In the same year as my previous quotation Marx wrote of the necessary contribution which capitalism had made to the creation of the modern working class and the cutting of 'the umbilical cord which still bound the worker of yesterday to the land and the soil'.[2] The third main influence on the young Marx was his observation of the life of the revolutionary socialists in Paris. This confirmed his belief that the historical sequence must be from the rural to the industrial, a revolution enabled by capitalism, which by socialism would be transformed into true humanism. This insistence on a pattern which had as yet only taken place in Europe was echoed by Engels soon after the death of Marx when he claimed 'that any revolution must be European if it is to triumph'.[3] It must therefore always be surprising that Third World countries should be influenced by a writer so critical of what he regarded as the deficiencies of rural life. As early as *The Communist Manifesto* Marx was praising capitalism because it 'rescued a considerable part of the population from the idiocy of rural life'.[4] And yet, as I have pointed out, the irony is that Marxism has been much more influential in the Third World countries than in the very Europe which Engels saw as the model for all development.

Nor was the philosophy of Marx, when rediscovered, influential on the USA. The reason, I believe, is that unlike Western European countries, the USA saw the Cold War as an ideological conflict, in which were at stake meaning, value, and the manifest destiny of the American people. In such circumstances it was not possible to adopt a pragmatic approach to Marx, using those parts which seemed valuable, rejecting those things which intervening history had falsified. As a result America denied itself the new critical philosophy at a time when social life urgently required a critical perspective. Instead, America turned to Freud for its critical philosophy. Even Marcuse, whose neo-Marxism within the context of the transplanted Frankfurt School of Critical Theory aroused some interest among students in the late 1960s, made considerable use of Freud. It is of some significance that when Norman O. Brown wrote his Freudian work *Life Against Death* in 1959, the subtitle was 'The Psychoanalytical Meaning of History'. I believe that Freud was employed in America to deal with areas which in Europe were analysed through Marx, and that this had unfortunate consequences for critical thought in the USA. To give one example, the Freudian model leads to the assumption that the alienation of the individual stems from his or her inability to come to terms with external reality, as defined by society. Thus by definition society is in order as it is: it is the individual who must adjust. While in particular cases this might be so, it is a poor and incomplete model on which to base a critical analysis of modern industrial society. Needless to say it has made no impact on the Third World. It was left to the 'anti-psychiatry' of R. D. Laing and others to challenge the model, and perhaps more tellingly to novelists such as Doris Lessing in her *Briefing for a Descent into Hell*. In the first two chapters we found that neither feminist theology, nor black theology, had paid sufficient attention to the necessity of a critical theory on which to analyse sexism and racism. The fact that both of these theologies are almost exclusively American may go a long way to explain this deficiency.

It could not therefore have been predicted that the rediscovered philosophy of the young Marx would be in the long term of little influence in Europe, the immediate cultural context in which it first arose, of no influence whatsoever in America that country which in other respects has been much influenced by Europe generally and in intellectual matters by Germany in particular, but of great influence in the countries of the Third World so different culturally from Europe and in many cases at that pre-industrial pre-capitalist stage of development characterized by a level of consciousness which Marx was pleased to describe as 'idiocy'.

Something else, even less predictable, has been Marx's influence on theology, particularly in the Third World, and especially as we shall see in Latin America. Marx was not personally interested enough in religion to spend much time criticizing it, but he was concerned about religion as a social institution and, for example, about the influence which the church had on German life and thought. But because Stalin persecuted the churches both in the USSR and subsequently in satellite countries such as Poland, it was assumed during the Cold War period that Marx must have shared this fervent desire to rid the world of religion. However, one of the immediate consequences of the publication of Marx's works in the 1950s was the initiation of a Marxist-Christian dialogue. It was found that the young humanist Marx exposed and condemned the ideological legitimations performed by the churches on behalf of the ruling class. But many Christians were prepared to accept this criticism and take steps to end this travesty of religion. It was found that the young Marx was critical of several forms of communism prevalent in his own day, and that his objectives were not at all alien to Christian social teaching.

To understand why Marx's philosophy could be such an important factor in the development of Liberation Theology it is necessary to distinguish between the central place which critical thinking about religion played in the development of his work generally and the minor and peripheral place which criticizing religion occupied in his life. If this sounds paradoxical, a failure to make this distinction has perpetuated a confusion about Marx and consequently a suspicion towards those theologians who have made use of aspects of his thought. In the nineteenth century it was common for philosophers to have studied theology earlier in their careers. Thus the first two important critics of Hegel from within the Hegelian school mounted their critiques of Hegel in the course of dealing with theological topics. D. F. Strauss began the process with his *Life of Jesus Critically Examined* (1835). He had a considerable influence on his contemporary, Ludwig Feuerbach, for example in designating mankind (the species) as the true subject of the predicates of Christ. It was Feuerbach who taught Marx how to criticize Hegel, and in his early works Marx was full of praise for Feuerbach as the leading critical thinker of the period immediately following the death of Hegel. Since Feuerbach criticized Hegel in a work dealing with religion, *The Essence of Christianity* (1841), it was inevitable that Marx's own critical philosophy should begin with the critique of religion. However, as we shall see, this did not mean that Marx was interested in dealing with institutional forms of religion.

Feuerbach wished to mount a critique of Hegel's system of Absolute Idealism, and chose as his starting point the formation of human consciousness and in particular the formation of religious conscious-ness. The Christian religion had been so influential on the development of Hegel's system that Feuerbach rightly judged that his critique of religion would undermine this kind of idealism. Feuerbach's position in contrast was soon designated as materialism, but he did not deserve that accolade, and it was precisely on this point that Marx was eventually to part company with him. But at the outset Feuerbach gave Marx an important lead, especially in his projection theory of religion. 'Man – this is the mystery of religion – projects his being into objectivity, and then again makes himself an object of this projected image of himself, thus converted into a subject.'[5] The statement in fact tells us very little about religion. Since then historical anthropology and more recently phenomenology have been used to throw light on the origins and nature of religion and religions. Although Feuerbach was deeply concerned with religion and being religious he was not very illuminating on the subject. However, Marx quite correctly observed that Feuerbach was actually presenting a very fruitful model for the understanding of the development of human consciousness and indeed societal life. It is a theory of a dialectical movement of externalization, objectification and internationalization. Man has the capacity to conceive of ideals and to project them away from himself. They then take on objective form in the external world, in the form of institutions. Finally, these institutions come to have an independent reality over against the individual. They act back and control man's life. Feuerbach had provided the first example. Man conceives of the ideal of suffering love and projects it away from himself. It is objectified over against man as an attribute of God. It then exists independently of man. It belongs to God and not to man. Finally, it acts back in such a way that man's life is controlled by the commandments of God to love the neighbour. This proposition seemed reasonable to Marx and he simply took over Feuerbach's interpretation of religion. 'The basis of irreligious criticism is this: man makes religion; religion does not make man.'[6] But Marx was not interested in religion and took up Feuerbach's model only because he saw its wider application. Thus in the Introduction which he wrote to his 'Critique of Hegel's Philosophy of Law' he began with these words: 'For Germany, the criticism of religion has been largely completed; and the criticism of religion is the premise of all criticism.'[7] The critique of religion was not the end of his task, but the beginning; with it he had not discovered the goal but rather the tool with which to begin his real work. 'This state, this society, produce religion which is an inverted world consciousness, because they are an inverted world.'[8] The world is distorted and man is alienated, but not because of religion. The reversal of reality observed in the case of religion is but an illustration of the fact that the whole social view of the world is an inverted form of consciousness. Thus the critique of religion solves no problems. Religion is not fundamental to Marx because it is only one among many instances of a deeper tendency to false consciousness. The exposing of religion does not produce true consciousness; it merely clears the decks for the real work of transformation. 'It is the task of history, therefore, once the other-world of truth has vanished, to establish the truth of this world. The immediate task of philosophy, which is in the service of history, is to unmask human self-alienation in its secular form now that it has been unmasked in its sacred form.'⁹ Thus Marx set out to expose the secular roots of alienation. In Hegel's philosophy human ideas of order and purpose had become objectified in the absolute Spirit which was being incarnated in the course of human history, controlling individual lives. The State itself which arose from man's ideals of justice had become independent, standing over against man. In religion man the creator had forgotten the process by which he created God, so now in political life the State granted or withheld rights of citizenship and enforced control of individuals by penalty of the courts or threat of the military. In his treatment of money we can see just how deeply Marx was indebted in his critical philosophy to Feuerbach's treatment of religion. 'Money is the universal and self-sufficient value of all things. It has, therefore, deprived the whole world, both the human world and nature, of their own proper value. Money is the alienated essence of man's work and existence; this essence dominates him and he worships it.'¹⁰

The nature of the paradox should now be clear. The criticism of religion was important to Marx, not as a criticism of religion, religions or religious institutions, but because it provided the model by which he could unmask the false consciousness surrounding the secular in-stitutions such as the state, money, labour and private property. Feuerbach was so obsessed with religion that he never progressed beyond his initial critique. Marx had no sympathy with this position since, as we have seen, religion was not the cause of alienation, nor did the setting aside of religion in itself achieve anything. Those who make the attack on religion a central issue have not understood Marx. He explains this point in rather Hegelian language. 'Atheism, as a denial of this unreality, is no longer meaningful, for atheism is a negation of God and seeks to assert by this negation the existence of man. Socialism no longer requires such a roundabout method.'¹¹ Which is just as well, since Marx's critique of religion is an instance of internal contradiction. In 1845 Marx jotted down eleven cryptic notes on Feuerbach, which he intended to elaborate in the form of discussion theses at some later date. These have come to be called the *Theses on Feuerbach* and, although never filled out, throw light on an important stage in the development of Marx's historical materialism. He came to see that Feuerbach was not after all a materialist. His work was still fundamentally guided by idealism, as was that of Strauss. 'The chief defect of all hitherto existing materialism – that of Feuerbach included – is that the thing, reality, sensuousness, is conceived only in the form of the object of contemplation, but not as sensuous human activity, practice, not subjectively.'[12] This was the parting of the ways with Feuerbach. But Marx omitted to note that he had actually taken over Feuerbach's critique of religion, which well illustrated the point at issue. Feuerbach had not in fact taken religion as his subject – objective, historical religion and religions in all their sensuous modes and expressions of praxis. Instead he had considered only the idea of religion, an abstract conception of it. Marx was entirely justified in criticizing Feuerbach for not dealing with the real religious life of people in their social world, but he did not return to the critique of religion to re-examine it in its proper context. Thus although Marx subjected all other social institutions to his historical materialist analysis, he never offered a scientific study of religion. It is therefore not at all impossible for theologians to use Marx's critical philosophy to gain an understanding of the social, political and economic formations in contemporary society. Marx's critique of religion rested on premises which he soon came to reject.

Original thinkers are not original in all things. Freud's anthropological studies on the origins of religion were wilful and historically unfounded even in his own day. Wittgenstein's remarks on religion are largely trivial. And yet those who have a genuine understanding of religion can derive great benefit from applying the general theories of such critical thinkers to their own subject. We might draw a parallel and say that the relevance of Marx for religion lies not in the specific remarks which he made on the subject, distributed throughout his works, but rather in the application of his general critical theories to the subject by experts in religion. Our immediate context is domination and liberation and it is possible to use Marx's general theory of alienation to expose the ways in which religion has contributed to oppression. More importantly it may be that Marx will also be suggestive when we ask how religion can contribute to the ending of alienation and the achievement of the truly human life. None of this is dependent on the validity of Marx's specific theory of religion, still less on his personal atheism. According to the

Mexican philosopher and theologian, José Miranda, after 1850 Marx no longer made an issue of atheism. Indeed, when questioned about religion in an interview in 1871 he deliberately distinguished the position of the International from his personal views. 'On that point I cannot speak in the name of the society. I myself am an atheist.'[3] The implication would seem to be that atheism was a personal matter, not a condition for the acceptance of his general critical philosophy.

We should therefore expect that Liberation Theology has been deeply influenced by Marx's critical philosophy, though not his specific comments on religion or his personal atheism. Although Liberation Theology is widely used throughout the Third World, more in Asia than in Africa, it is originally associated with Latin America, and for the sake of coherence we shall concentrate on examples from that area. One of the characteristics of Marxist analysis is the concept of class. Alienation is related fundamentally to the oppression of the vast majority (in Third World countries) by institutions controlled by and for the interests of the ruling class. I shall therefore examine the work of Latin American theologians writing on the oppression of the poor and class domination. But first we should consider how Marx's philosophy has led Latin American theologians to adopt a new method of doing theology which they contrast with the traditional method of European theology. Method might not seem the most interesting point at which to enter the subject of Liberation Theology, but as we shall see it is of crucial importance. Although those who begin to study a new subject immediately adopt a particular method, they are not aware of this issue until much later. The question of how to proceed is a very sophisticated question which only emerges as individuals master the field and in doing so become dissatisfied with the traditional approach. Living outside our own culture for a time can provide us with a valuable critical distance which enables us to uncover and question assumptions which we have taken for granted. It is not altogether surprising, therefore, that the criticism of the traditional theological method has come not from within Europe but from the Third World. Young scholars from Latin America who had mastered the subject as presented to them in their own countries were often sent abroad, to complete their graduate studies in Europe, very often in cities historically associated with the missionary movements which originally brought Christianity to their lands. At Rome or Louvain, Göttingen or Edinburgh, they were encouraged to continue what they had already proved that they could do well. And when they returned home what more natural than that they should continue to write articles and books which contributed to European debates? If the question of method did arise, then it was a choice between Harnack and Barth, Tillich and Bultmann, or perhaps a reinforcement of rejecting Modernism and maintaining Thomism. But from the perspective of the Third World the best of the young theologians were dissatisfied with these options, perceiving within them presuppositions which they could not accept. What if all of these options – regardless of their considerable differences – should depend on assumptions which are so much a part of Western culture that they are simply taken for granted? And what if that should become clear not to those continuing to live within that culture, but to those who, while perfectly familiar with it, have returned to a social world in which such things are no longer taken for granted, but are now seen to be deeply contentious. In Edinburgh in 1910 it became clear that the mission churches had certain things fundamentally in common with each other which alienated them from the old religious divisions of Europe. After the Second Vatican Council it appeared that theologians of Latin America, Catholic and Protestant, had certain things fundamentally in common which alienated them from the common assumptions of their founder churches in Europe. The fact that these theologians have now substantially departed from the European tradition is not at all through ignorance or lack of training. On the contrary, they are so well equipped that they are free to expose and criticize what they take to be the inadequacies of European theology. Liberation Theology is not the application of traditional theology to a different agenda including exotic phenomena such as revolution. It is theology done through a completely different method, and this transformation has been in large part brought about by the application of certain insights from Marx. This can be illustrated in the work of Jon Sobrino, a Jesuit who teaches in El Salvador, especially *The True Church and the Poor* (= *TC*).

It might be as well to state the obvious at the outset, that Liberation Theology is Christian theology and as such shares a fundamental faith with European theology. 'For freedom Christ has set us free . . .' (Galatians 5.1). All Christian theologies share this faith, that Christ in his person and work comes as liberator. But how that liberation is conceived, and how theology can represent and even promote it, is subject to profound differences. In a lecture given in 1975 Sobrino contrasts European and Latin American theologies by reference to the Enlightenment. The eighteenth century saw religion enter a new and rather humbling relationship with the modern age. Or rather, since institutionally religion continued to maintain a considerable influence on society, we should say that theology found itself confronted by autonomous reason. With a new confidence stemming from initial successes in the natural sciences and mathematics, reason set itself up as the arbiter of all knowledge. It was not always irreligious, but took special pleasure in putting religion in its place. We might say that it took as its motto, but with a certain abrasiveness, the ancient aphorism of Protagoras, 'Man is the measure of all things, of the reality of those which are, and the unreality of those which are not.'[14] If religion wished to be taken seriously, then theologians had to appear before the bar of reason to show that religious beliefs were rational. The grounds of religion must be justifiable to historical reason, in the form of the new historical criticism. And theology was also required to show that the content of religion added to human knowledge, that is, that it was compatible with the findings of the sciences. Since the Enlightenment claimed that man is liberated by reason, theology since the eighteenth century has been intent on showing that it contributes to this liberation of the mind. To perform these functions theology has to be closely associated with philosophy, and inevitably becomes a highly rational and intellectual discipline. It is always under pressure, and its agenda tends to be set for it by the challenges of autonomous reason.

As if that were not enough, in the nineteenth and twentieth centuries theology has been required to perform yet another function. During this period the increasingly secular European culture, itself in large part the outcome of the Enlightenment, has experienced a crisis of meaning. Nietzsche was the most perceptive observer of the crumbling of the religious foundations of modern culture. He described the process in the metaphor of the 'death of God'. The liberal tradition, from Schleiermacher onwards, undertook to show that man's life can only be meaningfully understood from a religious perspective. Neo-orthodoxy, under Barth, attempted to show why man's life without (the Christian) religion was necessarily meaningless. But in this they were agreed, that theology should provide an interpretation of man and the world which was superior to any interpretation without reference to God. Once again the requirements of reason, in this case the need for meaning, set the agenda, and theology was confirmed as a highly intellectual discipline.

It is along these lines that Sobrino characterizes European theology, both Catholic and Protestant. It is a child of the Enlightenment as represented by Kant. Theology wishes to be compatible with reason, but has no aspirations to criticize reason. Perhaps surprisingly Sobrino does not mention Hegel, who has been so influential on the development of the social sciences. In a famous aphorism Hegel claimed that 'What is real is rational, and what is rational is real'.[15] His philosophy had the effect of showing that what is is what should be, and that behind or beyond the contradictions of our experience of the world there is a more profound understanding which when eventually revealed will disclose their true meaning. To this extent, modern theology has assisted Hegel in the attempt to interpret the contradictions of life. According to Sobrino this is how modern European theology understands itself and its function, and herein lies the fundamental contrast with the Liberation Theology of Latin America.

Latin American theology is also a child of the Enlightenment, but Sobrino relates it to Marx rather than Kant. This tradition does not believe that man will be liberated simply by reason, by avoiding intellectual errors or by understanding the world better. These things are necessary, but not enough. According to Marx man is not puzzled by the world, but oppressed in it. He is not so much the victim of error as of evil. The goal of Marx's philosophy is therefore the liberation of man, but his critical philosophy employs reason not simply to understand the world, but to expose the world for what it is. According to Sobrino Latin American theology belongs to this tradition. He is therefore claiming that it refuses to assume the reasonableness of the world as it is. Nor does it accept the role of providing an interpretation of the world as it is. Here of course we see the influence of Marx's XIth Thesis on Feuerbach: 'The philosophers have only interpreted the world, in various ways, the point is to change it.'[16] Marx is here criticizing Feuerbach, and beyond that Hegel's confidence in the reasonableness of the present order of things. In like manner, Latin American theology refuses to legitimize an unjust and oppressive system. Liberation comes not from understanding injustice, but through bringing it to an end. 'The theological concern is not to explain as accurately as possible what the essence of sin is, or what meaning a sinful world has, or what meaning human existence has in such a world. The concern is to change the sinful situation.'[17] This is not reason, but critical reason. Such a theology is not concerned to understand the world as it is, but to expose how the world is. It is not concerned to find meaning in a world which has no meaning because of its contradictions and patent absurdity. The European Economic Community has produced huge food surpluses in recent years at precisely the same time as the worst famines in modern times in Ethiopia and Sudan. Explanations can be given of the food mountains, even reasons for them. But should theology ally itself with the rationality of such a world or should it seek to put the world on a new footing? Or to approach the matter from a different angle, European theology has always been concerned with suffering. How is it possible to reconcile human suffering with the omnipotent God of love? Theology is here concerned not with suffering, but with the idea of suffering. Latin American theology does not seek an interpretation of suffering which accounts for suffering and gives it its place in the scheme of things. The problem of suffering is not understanding it, but identifying its causes and eliminating them.

In a long series of B-movies about Africa under the British Empire, as the drums beat in the darkness white settlers would say to each other, 'The natives are restless tonight, Carruthers'. It was assumed if the natives were restless, there must be something wrong with the natives, not the empire. In Britain today a whole generation of young people is growing up without any opportunity of creative work. Is it theology's task to provide meaning for lives which are inherently meaningless? This would be to fulfil exactly the role which Marx assigned to religion, to make the intolerable tolerable. According to the Latin American view it is not for theology to provide an interpretation of the meaningless, but to challenge the rationality of such a system. It is for this reason that as European theology is closely related to philosophy – which explains why the world is as it is – so Latin American theology seeks assistance from the social sciences. A theology which is responsible for exposing and condemning the ills of society and advocating a new order must understand why things are as they are and how they might be changed. We noted already that the agenda for theology in Europe is set for it by the challenge of reason, of Enlightenment philosophy and science. In contrast, the agenda for Latin American theology is set by the suffering of the poor. Sobrino quotes Berdyaev with approval. 'If I go hungry it is a physical evil; if others go hungry it is a moral evil' (*TC*, 28). He concludes, 'In the face of moral evil there is only one proper response: get rid of it' (*TC*, 28). From this it is clear that the method of this theology has not been established on purely intellectual grounds. Circumstances have forced theologians to address practical issues, and this in turn has led to considered action, i.e. praxis. They do not begin with revealed truths which must be reconciled with actual situations. 'The reflection that suffering stimulates is not essentially an effort to explain the nature of suffering or to investigate its compatibility with the data of revelation; it is an effort to eliminate the suffering' (*TC*, 29).

A final example of the way in which European theology has been formed by the Enlightenment concerns theodicy, the problem of reconciling God and the injustice of the world. Theodicy falls within the general area of the problem of God. The issue is raised in the Bible in the context of the life of faith, but in modern times it is an intellectual problem. The difficulty in answering the problem seems almost a scandal to philosophical theology. But not to Latin American theology, 'since the basic scandal is not that evil exists despite the fact that God exists, but simply that evil exists' (*TC*, 30). In European theology the most extreme expression of the problem of God was in the 'death of God'. Unfortunately it is not at all melodramatic to say that in Latin America theology has had to focus on the death of man, the death of the peasant, the poor, the oppressed and those who had identified with them. 'In Latin America death does not mean simply the disappearance of that which had supposedly given meaning to things (in this case, God), but the triumph of injustice and sin' (*TC*, 32). Religion is not challenged here by irreligion but evil. 'The enemy of theology has been less the atheist than the inhuman' (*TC*, 37).

According to Sobrino we are dealing with two completely different perspectives on theology, exemplified in their now radically opposed methods, functions and objectives. Small wonder that Latin American theologians have become disenchanted with European theology. They see the connection between European theology and Europe's understanding of itself as being at the centre of the world. 'European theology is trying (admittedly in goodwill) to reconcile the wretched state of the real world at the level of theological thought, but it is not trying to liberate the real world from its wretched state' (*TC*, 18). The new method and its critique of the old method are deeply indebted to the perspectives provided by the early Marx. The most obvious point of contact is with the XIth Thesis on Feuerbach, but the difference between the two methods might also be seen as an illustration of Marx's fundamental point about the reversal of reality. As noted earlier Marx exposed a tendency to false consciousness which characterizes the individual's relationship to social institutions. The institution, although socially constructed, appears to the individual to be part of the natural order of things. Its existence is taken for granted and its form of existence controls the consciousness and the life of the individual within the sphere of its influence. Feuerbach was a critic not of religion but of theology, and it is theology as much as religion which Marx criticizes. Could we then apply this reversal of reality theory to theology? Theology would then indeed be a socially constructed phenomenon, which although not part of the natural world seems to the individual believer to be permanent and to be taken for granted. Theology would be an example of something man-made which now assumes independent existence and acts back to control both thought and behaviour. European theology would on this view provide an explanation or legitimation of how the world is. It would not challenge how the world is, but much more importantly, if actual experience contradicted theology, so much the worse for experience. Theology would give a picture of how things really are – if we could only see as God sees. When in *The German Ideology* Marx claimed that 'Life is not determined by consciousness, but consciousness by life',[18] he was asserting that this is what should be the case. Our consciousness should be determined by our experience. The way we live our lives responsibly should spring from our experience of living. Marx was rejecting the more familiar process by which how we live our lives is determined by some already existing system of beliefs and values, be it an ideology or a theology, which is not correctible by experience. What Sobrino characterizes as European or traditional theology is such an already existing religious world view. Its accuracy and truth are already established. Such a theology is incorrigible. If our experience contradicts this theology, then it can only be because through sin or sloth we have not understood reality as disclosed by theology. The theology which Sobrino associates with Latin America is not already existing. It actually arises as a second-order discipline from the experience of the people of God. Such a theology will not insist that relationships within a nation or relationships among nations are essentially in order. It will arise from the experience of injustice and will therefore seek to expose and condemn and therefore bring to an end injustice within or among nations.

This leads on to another important distinction between the old and new theologies. We have already noted that for Sobrino, the focus of Liberation Theology is the oppression of one class by another, the poor by the rich, the weak by the powerful. By now we see that the new theology is not simply reflecting on the situation of the oppressed class: it arises from the experience of the oppressed. In *The German Ideology* Marx goes on to say that, 'The ideas of the ruling class are in every epoch the ruling ideas, i.e. the class which is the ruling material force in society, is at the same time its ruling intellectual force.'[19] What we see in Liberation Theology is the transition from a theology which expresses the perspectives of the ruling class and serves its interests to a theology which is derived from the perspectives of the oppressed class. The difference is that this theology is not to be used for the advantage of the oppressed but rather for the ending of all oppression. This is why Liberation Theology is primarily a theology of liberation: that is its goal.

The new theology cannot therefore be a variation of the old theology. It cannot be carried out, for example, by European theologians thinking about the oppressed of the Third World. Nor can it be the application of the old theology by those of whom we have already spoken, who finished their training in Europe and returned to Latin America. It is not a theology about the oppressed, but a theology of the oppressed. And if this seems unjustified or unlikely, it is surely no more objectionable than the unqualified promise, 'Blessed are you poor, for yours is the kingdom of God' (Luke 6.20). The Uruguayan Methodist theologian Julio de Santa Ana undertook a study of 'The Church and the Poor' on behalf of the World Council of Churches' Commission on the Churches' Participation in Development. The first volume was published under the title *Good News to the Poor: the Challenge of the Poor in the History of the Church* (= *GN*), and dealt with biblical material as well as the period of the early church. He came to the conclusion that 'in the Old Testament poverty is considered an evil, as a constant painful fact, whose consequences are the establishment of relationships of dependence and oppression . . .'[20] The prophets denounce such situations, and in the Pentateuch there is detailed legislation intended to prevent accumulation of wealth and resultant exploitation (*GN*, 6). We see the same perspective outlined above when he says that 'this struggle to eradicate poverty makes it clear that it is not a matter of explaining how things come about . . .' (*GN*, 6). In the Old Testament it is commonly assumed that while the rich man is self-sufficient, the poor can only look to God for help. It is they who, in the Gospels, have good news preached to them (Matthew 11.5). It is worth having before us again the report of the first sermon of Jesus, referred to in the second lecture. Jesus chooses the text from Isaiah: 'The Spirit of the Lord is upon me, because he has anointed me to preach good news to the poor. He has sent me to proclaim release to the captives and recovering of sight to the blind, to set at liberty those who are oppressed, to proclaim the acceptable year of the Lord.' Just as the text cannot be passed over by those who are captive and enslaved, so in our present context it cannot be passed over in a world so deeply divided as ours into ruling classes and ruled, oppressors and oppressed, rich and poor. It is not a text which legitimizes the present arrangements. As Santa Ana points out, 'the text emphasized what we might call the *privilege of the poor* (*GN*, 13). But the privilege is that God's judgment is coming and with it the end of oppression and the suffering of the poor. The poor are not blessed because of some virtue or moral status. '*This poverty is not a virtue but an evil* which constitutes a challenge to the justice of the Lord who is King of creation' (*GN*, 17). Poverty is therefore not extolled as an ideal for Christians: it is exposed as evil and Christians must take responsibility for alleviating it. What will be the basis of God's judgment? 'Truly, I say to you, as you did it not to one of the least of these, you did it not to me' (Matt. 25.45). These were to become the alternatives within the church as it developed. On the one hand there was the monastic and ascetic voluntary poverty as an ideal. On the other there was the norm of charity: 'blessed are the poor' gradually became 'blessed are those who give to the poor'. In neither case was the good news of Jesus preserved. Santa Ana notes a work by the French Dominican Benoit Dumas, who spent some years working in Uruguay, on the challenging theme of *ubi Christus ibi ecclesia*. There is a danger that if Christ says he is with the poor, and the church is not with the poor, then it will not be the true church. This is a theme taken up by Sobrino in the remainder of his book *The True Church and the Poor*.

Sobrino emphasizes the point made by Santa Ana concerning the 'privilege of the poor'. 'God's manifestation, at least in Latin America, is his scandalous and partisan love for the poor and his intention that these poor should receive life and thus inaugurate his kingdom.'[21] The older theology, if it thought about such matters, probably assumed that God belonged with the ruling classes, but as a benevolent being he was kindly disposed towards the poor. But if the example of Jesus is normative for our understanding of God, then God has taken sides in the class conflict and has pitched his tent with those who suffer unjustly and are oppressed. Whenever theology adopts the even-handed approach of bourgeois liberalism then God somehow ends up on the side of those who define and control things as they are. The new theology cannot be even-handed in such matters. Sobrino continues the quotation, 'Correspondingly, the proper way of being conformed to God is to be concerned actively with the justice of the kingdom of God and with making the poor the basis of this concern.' Sobrino is not of course rejecting theology or the church, but is concerned rather that if a line is drawn through society between the classes they should be found on the same side as God. God is not above or beyond the conflict. As Miranda puts it, 'The question is not whether someone is seeking God or not, but whether he is seeking him where God himself said that he is.'[22] Where

Christ is, there is the true church: but where has Christ said he will be? Does the church already possess God, and make him available to the poor? Or rather is God already with the poor in such a way that they are now the criterion of the church? 'For the poor pose the problem of seeking God without presupposing that the church possesses him once and for all. At the same time they offer the church the place for finding him' (*TC*, 93). There is here the reversal so typical of the gospel itself. Sobrino quotes a saying circulating in Latin America: 'the poor evangelize the church' (*TC*, 121). Can he be serious? How can the poor without any training or resources evangelize the great institution which has been the preserver, transmitter and communicator of the gospel? But as we have seen, in the Beatitudes the poor are not singled out because of their own virtues. 'There is no question of idealizing, much less sacralizing the poor' (*TC*, 95). We have already noted the alternative developments in the church. The first was the choice of a life of poverty. But the poor do not choose to be poor: poverty is not a virtue for them but an evil. And those who choose poverty, especially within a financially secure religious institution, do not suffer the oppression experienced by the poor. The second approach was to pronounce blessed those who give to the poor. But by definition such alleviation is not intended to defeat the evil of poverty or to eliminate it from society. Sobrino claims that the poor raise the question about the true church. They are the criterion, but not when the church adopts poverty voluntarily or when it acts in charity towards the poor. 'But in principle a church *for* the poor is not yet a church *of* the poor' (*TC*, 92). While the church is maintained on the side of the ruling class, acting with charity towards the oppressed, the evil of class domination is not addressed, let alone exposed or opposed.

What is at stake here is the nature of the church. Even the desire to help the poor does not extricate the church from its attachment to the ruling class and the influence of the models and presuppositions of that class. 'The church has been historically organized for example, on the basis of such facts as hierarchy or celibacy. As a result these facts of hierarchical power or celibate life have become historically primary facts on the basis of which both the totality of the church and the hierarchical ordering of its values have been understood historically. For example, if one accepted the hierarchy of the church as its primary ecclesial fact, then one would propose the use of authority and the demand for obedience as historical mediations for the experience of God' (*TC*, 135). Sobrino is making the important claim that as long as the church is organized according to the principles characteristic of the ruling class, even if its actions are directed to the alleviating of the plight of the poor, the church is not transformed. It is still on the wrong side of the line. It is not where God has declared that he will be found. Such a church is not undermining domination by class, but by the way in which it exercises even its charity, perpetuates and confirms the essential rightness of the values of the ruling class. Of course we are speaking here not of a God of natural theology, the theology which seems natural to the rulers of this world, but of the God revealed in the one who became a slave. 'We labour under the disadvantage of having inherited a God who is more Aristotelian than biblical' (*TC*, 297). Christ who pronounced the poor blessed did not exercise power in the mode of the oppressing class, even to help the victims. Nor did God intervene by decree to prevent the cross. 'A church *for* the poor is not yet necessarily a church *of* or *from* the poor. In such a church, the poor would not yet constitute a historical principle for the configuration of the church, even though they may very well be the principle recipients of the mission of the church' (*TC*, 135). The good news cannot be preached to the poor by a church which still relies on the wisdom of the rulers of this world in ordering its life. 'A true church of the poor must look at poverty from the perspective of the beatitudes. They propose in effect a salvific kenosis, which in order to be salvific must be a kenosis' (*TC*, 137). A church which daily relies on the structures which it shares with the oppressors cannot bring an experience of God to the poor. Sobrino's point is that if the church came to share the perspective of the poor, then there could be a resurrection of the church. 'Poverty, powerlessness, and persecution constitute the real and material conditions for a church in keeping with the will of God to arise and for the possibility of an experience of God within such an ecclesial channel to take place' (*TC*, 137).

Sobrino is clearly not confident of the outcome so far as the institutional church is concerned. After Vatican II the hierarchy in Latin America did begin to advocate the part of the poor, but the conference of bishops has been unwilling to apply the critique of oppression to the church itself: 'Medellin is now dying the death of a thousand qualifications and distinctions' (*TC*, 198). Or as Juan Segundo has put it: 'The bishops prescribe much more energetic remedies for society than for the church itself.'[23] It is hard to argue against ambulance work when faced with specific cases, but when we ask about the place of religion in class domination, then it may well be that exercise of charitable work by an institution which is itself based on models taken from the ideology of domination can only perpetuate domination. This theme has been pursued by the Brazilian theologian Leonardo Boff, not simply as a theoretical or theological matter, but in the light of the way in which he himself has suffered under the Curia.

If Latin American theologians had simply stopped at the point of criticizing theological method they would have attracted little attention abroad. And even a call for the church to be aligned with the poor would not have gone beyond what was already said by the bishops in conference. However, as we have seen, the criticism pressed on beyond method and charity, to the nature of the church itself. This brought a response from Rome. In August 1984 on the authority of the Pope a document was published by Cardinal Joseph Ratzinger, Prefect of the Congregation for the Doctrine of the Faith, a body previously called the Congregation of the Inquisition. It was entitled 'Instruction on Certain Aspects of the "Theology of Liberation"', and its purpose was as follows:

to draw the attention of pastors, theologians, and all the faithful to the deviations, and risks of deviation, damaging to the faith and to Christian living, that are brought about by certain forms of liberation theology which use, in an insufficiently critical manner, concepts borrowed from various currents of Marxist thought.[24]

It was widely believed that although he was not mentioned by name, the Instruction was issued against the views of the Franciscan Leonardo Boff, especially a work originally published in Brazil in 1981, and translated under the title *Church, Charism and Power: Liberation Theology and the Institutional Church* (= *CCP*).[25] Boff was summoned to Rome to answer questions concerning his book. However, far from appearing as a heretic for the burning, he arrived in Rome flanked by two Brazilian cardinals and bearing a long and detailed reply to the original questions raised against him. The four-hour session was inconclusive, but later Boff was banned from teaching or publicizing his views. Boff might well have taken this experience as confirmation of the central thesis of his book. The church, instead of providing an alternative to the worldly structures of domination, actually practises the oppression of the weak by the powerful, the ruled by the rulers.

We need not enter here into a detailed examination of the criticisms of Boff offered by the Instruction,[26] but they make strange reading. It is obviously too late to suppress Liberation Theology. It cannot be discredited as the work of a few mad monks or some unfrocked priests.

But if it is here to stay, it must be controlled from the centre. The Congregation must now define what Liberation Theology really is, and, just as important, must indicate that it is not at all new, but has been part of the teaching of the church, held everywhere, always and by all. In the light of Sobrino's criticism of the European theological tradition, this attempted take-over would seem to be without foundation. The Instruction presents Jesus Christ as Liberator (the very title of one of Boff's earlier works) and affirms the church's commitment to the rights of the poor. 'The scandal of the shocking inequality between rich and poor – whether between rich and poor countries, or betwen social classes in a single nation – is no longer tolerated.' And yet this affirmation simply identifies the church as a church *for* the poor, not a church *of* the poor, to use Sobrino's terminology. The Instruction goes on to condemn the uncritical appropriation of Marxist analysis, assumptions about the social nature of evil, the inevitability of class struggle and the necessity of revolution. If there are theologians in Latin America who have swallowed this kind of Marxism, Sobrino and Boff are certainly not among them. Boff uses certain aspects of Marxist analysis in his criticism of the institutional church, the church centred in Rome and well represented by the Congregation for the Doctrine of the Faith. It is difficult to resist the conclusion that he has been singled out for such treatment, not because of his advocacy of liberation or even his use of Marxist analysis, but because of the profound, alarming and penetrating criticism which he makes of the Roman church. He both extends and sharpens Sobrino's claim that far from offering liberation to the captive and good news to the poor, the Roman church is inherently oppressive and can only serve to perpetuate domination throughout the world.

Boff begins from a position similar to that of Sobrino. Society is divided into social classes, and the question is, how does the church relate to this situation? Does it stand over against society as a witness to another and better way, or is it conformed to society? Of course the church institutes programmes of assistance and relief for the poor, 'leading the church to become a church *for* the poor rather than a church *with* or *of* the poor' (*CCP*, 4). Once again we see the church presented as an institution which is modelled on the structures of domination on which society operates. The church has no difficulty in relating to other centres of power and domination. 'This type of church, founded upon priestly and magisterial power as well as the sacred authority of the hierarchy conforms to the centralist policies of Rome' (*CCP*, 5). When it is bestowing charity upon the poor, it does so from a sphere outside of that class. The church's 'relationship with the poor will thus be defined from the perspective of the rich; the rich will be called upon to aid the cause of the poor, but without necessarily requiring a change in social class practice' (*CCP*, 7). Boff is claiming that even when the church seems to be taking up the case of the poor, it does not do so in such a way as to call in question the basis of the class society and its inherent injustice. 'In every other case the church appears to be conformable with authoritarian régimes; it never questions their legitimacy, only their abuses' (*CCP*, 5). Clearly, then, Boff is accusing the church of taking its place within the ruling class. Neither its occasional criticisms of the rich nor its charitable work among the poor challenge the relationships which are determined by the class structure. But already Boff is saying something more than that, more important and incisive. His criticism is not so much that the church exists *in* a class society, as that the church itself *is* a class society. Not that the church co-exists within a class society, but that the church replicates the class society. Not that the church fails to criticize the values on which society is founded, but that the church also exists on the same basis. 'The power structure in the church today is indebted to centuries-old patterns, and two patterns are worth noting in particular: the experience with Roman power and the feudal structure. The church assumed customs, titles, expressions, and symbols from them' (*CCP*, 40). Internal criticism which was still possible at the Reformation was ended with the excommunication of Luther, Boff claims, with a further advance towards domination within. 'Catholicism became a total, reactionary, violent, and repressive ideology. There is nothing further from the evangelical spirit than the catholicistic system's pretension to unlimited infallibility, to unquestionability, to absolute certainty (*CCP*, 86). As Boff describes it, it is not difficult to see why the church's occasional criticisms of the ruling class do not challenge the common assumptions about the uses of power, and why the church's activities on behalf of the poor do not alter the relationships which maintain oppression. He comes to the following conclusion. 'It is strange to see that the church institution has developed into exactly that which Christ did not want it to be: from the will for power, hierarchies of teachers, doctors, fathers, fathers of fathers, and servants of servants have all arisen' (*CCP*, 60).

It might have been of some comfort to the Congregation for the Doctrine of the Faith if Boff, having made such criticisms, had then left the church. The conclusion would have been obvious, and indeed his departure would have provided further confirmation of the essential rightness of things within the church. But Boff has not left the church. Worse than that, his criticisms of the institutional church, the Roman church, arise not from historical or theoretical studies, but from practical experience. Boff writes from his participation in the *comunidades eclesiales de base*. This is usually translated as 'basic Christian communities', but that does not bring out their fundamental characteristic. If the Roman church is hierarchical, characterized by that chain of command from the Pope through the cardinals, bishops, priests which impinges on the laity at the base of the pyramid, these new Christian communities are composed by those who live at the base. A community is typically fifteen or twenty families, meeting weekly to hear the word of God, and to share their lives and their problems. When Boff was writing the book there were already some 70,000 such groups in Brazil. Although basically comprised of the poor and the most oppressed class, they have been joined by others, including priests, bishops and even cardinals. There is no alienation from the church: this development is within the church but it is a new experience of being the church. The cardinals who accompanied Boff to Rome were by their presence affirming that he writes what many have experienced. The charisms, the gifts of the Spirit of which Paul wrote are present in these communities of service and of hope. Boff is so clear about the nature of the institutional church because he has experienced in the base communities non-dominant relationships, sharing of responsibilities and decision-making, common power which is used in service. The communities are not political cells, but they transform the consciousness of the people who participate, assisting them to see through the ideology of domination and enabling them to avoid repeating the pattern of oppression. 'The base community does not become a political entity. It remains what is is: a place for the reflection and celebration of faith. But, at the same time it is the place where human situations are judged ethically in the light of God' (*CCP*, 9). Boff has no intention of leaving the church. It is because he has participated in a new form of the church that he can now criticize the institutional church. If one is precisely the opposite of the early church, the other has many of the characteristics of the primitive community. If one participates in domination and promotes it, the other rejects domination and promotes liberation. The church, instead of being a light to the world, has been a mirror, reflecting the structures of oppression. It is in this sense that the poor evangelize the church. Those who have been oppressed understand but reject this way of proceeding. It would not be difficult to draw a comparison here with another theme from the early Marx. When Marx asked where there was any sign or possibility of liberation in Germany he concluded that there was no hope in individuals or existing groups at that time. Liberation could only come from a new class. What is of particular interest is that he was not able to speak about this new sphere of society without using terminology which is deeply Christian. He spoke of 'a sphere, finally, which cannot emancipate itself without emancipating itself from all other spheres of society, without, therefore, emancipating all these other spheres, which is, in short, a total loss of humanity and which can only redeem itself by a *total redemption of humanity*. This dissolution of society, as a particular class, is the proletariat.'[27] This important though enigmatic passage must suggest to Christians the model of the Suffering Servant and of the figure of Christ. The poor evangelize the church. Only those who are oppressed can bring oppression to an end. They cannot do it by becoming oppressors and exchanging places, reducing others to their former state. That way oppression has the victory. It can only be brought to an end by those who refuse to allow it to continue in their own lives. If Marx is in any sense justified in speaking of a total redemption of humanity, it must mean that it is by the suffering of the oppressed that finally oppression is ended and both oppressors and oppressed are united. Whether Marx was fortunate enough to glimpse this in any group in the course of his life we do not know, but Boff clearly has: a church of those who are oppressed but by refusing to aspire to become oppressors might by the grace of God assist in the redemption of the church, and the world.

Perhaps we should finish on this high note: we have after all examined the place of religion in domination and liberation in the particular context of class conflict. However, there is more to be said and it has significance not only for this context but for the other two with which we have so far dealt. In the first two chapters I said that feminist theologians and black theologians lacked social theory, a critical analysis of domination based on gender and race. In particular I underlined the tendency of feminists to think that when domination was uncovered it would somehow die of shame. But domination continues right along even when exposed. Why is this? Because men are evil and white people are evil? But that does not reach to the heart of the problem. Why do people continue to dominate and oppress even when they have no desire or wish to do so? It is at this point that the

Latin Americans, in this case Boff, exhibit the necessity of a critical analysis which goes beyond simple observation.

The stage we have reached is that Boff is describing a new movement within the church which is well placed to expose domination within society at large, and also the way in which the institutional church participates in oppression on its own account. On the feminist model we should then expect the base communities to call on the institution to stop its domination. Now that oppression has been uncovered and exposed, surely it will not continue? But of course it will continue. The institutional church shows no sign of changing its ways. The answer might be that the people who are in charge of the institution are unworthy, and have no desire to give up a system which suits them very well. In particular cases this might well be so, just as particular men continue to dominate women and particular white people continue to oppress blacks. But it is at this point that we need some more comprehensive approach to the problem. The attribution of evil intent does not exhaust the possibilities and does not take us beyond the surface of the issue. Nothing would have been easier for Boff than to attribute his treatment to malevolence on the part of those in positions of power within the church. If only that were the case! If only the problem was as simple and easily dealt with as that! It is ironic that in the book, written before the summons to Rome, Boff actually includes the name of Joseph Ratzinger among those who like himself are committed to a historical-critical approach to theological matters rather than a purely dogmatic view. The oppression of individuals or groups (classes) within the church cannot be explained by maligning those in high office. If the human rights of individuals are violated, then this cannot be attributed 'to human deficiencies of those in authority in the church' (*CCP*, 59). That approach would be to assume that the structures of the church are in order but are subverted by evil men. For Boff this not only is quite untrue and unworthy, but actually gets the problem round the wrong way. 'But we must remember that the majority of those in authority in the church are men of good faith, clear conscience, impeccable personal character. The problem lies on a deeper level, on the structure that to a great degree is independent of persons' (*CCP*, 39). This is the most damning criticism yet made. The church exists in a class society. The church co-exists with the dominant class. The church participates in the same domination characteristic of a class society. Serious criticisms, but at the end it is always possible for those who do not make a dogma of the perfection of the church, to admit that things can go wrong within it. But

Boff has now pressed beyond the point at which even this concession is enough. He is claiming that the structures of the church are such that they produce evil even when operated by men of integrity and impeccable character. A hierarchical institution is so constituted that it promotes the interests of those in power at the expense of those without power. This domination is not an aberration or a misuse of the system. On the contrary, that is how it works when it runs properly. Ironically, in the hands of those of great virtue and integrity, it is guaranteed to dominate the weak to the advantage of the powerful. It is so constituted that men who are themselves incorruptible will deal harshly with any who challenge or attempt to frustrate the operation of the system. 'Every institution runs these risks and has the tendency to become autocratic, that is, to become a system of power and repression over creativity and criticism' (*CCP*, 48). If only violations of human rights could be attributed to a misuse of a system which otherwise would protect the poor and the weak! But what is to be done when domination and oppression are the results of the system when it is operated with the greatest integrity? 'There are violations of human rights within the church itself. These are not those abuses that are the result of individual abuses of power which are temporal in nature; we refer to those that are the result of a certain way of understanding and organizing the reality of the ecclesial structure – a somewhat permanent state of affairs' (*CCP*, 33).

Now we come to the heart of the problem. If domination takes place because of the evil actions of evil officials, the implication is that the institution is sound, if allowed to operate properly. But what if when the system is operated properly, according to its own premises, rules and values – when it is operated not by self-seeking or corrupt people, but by leaders of outstanding moral stature – what if in these, the best of all circumstances, it still even then produces domination? How are things to be changed? What if those who intend good nevertheless produce evil? It is here that Boff applies a further insight which he takes from Marx. Boff, in full flight, cannot take time to explain the social theory which he uses, but it is worth elaborating the argument which lies behind his assertions.

Earlier we noted that Boff claimed that the church was influenced by the main features of the society in which it existed, examples being the ancient Roman and the mediaeval feudal. This may have reminded Boff of an important study by Marx on the formation of societies in various epochs. Marx traced the historical sequence. 'In broad outline, Asiatic, ancient, feudal and modern bourgeois modes of production can be designated as progressive epochs in the economic formation of society.'[28] This was an important stage in the development of Marx's historical materialism. He was offering an alternative account of social history. History is not governed by Providence, as if the unseen hand of God intervened constantly to control and correct, directing history in spite of man towards an eschatological goal. Nor, for Marx, was Hegel's proposal any better, in which the Absolute Spirit was becoming progressively incarnate and therefore revealed in human history. For Marx neither of these idealist accounts took proper cognizance of the material nature of man's social life. History is guided not by ideas but by activity, not by ideals but by labour. Social relations and therefore social institutions arise from the circumstances of production. For Marx history is therefore the history of successive modes of production, each epoch characterised by a different mode. 'The sum total of the relations of production constitutes the economic structure of society, the real foundation, on which rises a legal and political superstructure, and to which correspond definite forms of social consciousness. The mode of production of material life conditions the social, political and intellectual life process in general.'[29] Fundamental change in society, therefore, according to Marx, is brought about only by a change in the mode of production. The corollary is that it is not possible to change fundamentally the character of a society, or the relationships within it, without such a change in production. Hence of course his *magnum opus* dealt with captial. Capitalism, like every previous mode of production, determines the development of the institutions of society and relations within it. Returning to Boff, we have noted that he does not approach the church as an institution within a class society, but rather as itself an example of a class society. Our question is, how can the church change at a fundamental level? At this point Boff tells us, 'A premise taken here – and it is far too difficult to prove here – is that the organization of a society revolves around its means of production' (*CCP*, 110). But this premise is in fact Marx's theory of economic formations, to which I have just referred. At the outset Boff did not spend muct time criticizing the church for its activities within a class society, but went on to characterize it as itself an example of a class society. So in common with other liberation theologians, he could criticize the church's participation in capitalist society, but instead he goes on to the next stage. Not that the church exists within a capitalist society, but rather that the church is itself an example of a capitalist society.

If this seems unlikely, Boff goes on to spell out why it is nevertheless so. If the church is considered here not as an institution within a society, but as itself a society, then its development must be determined by its mode of production. As Boff describes it, the church is characterized by a form of religious monopoly capitalism (to coin a phrase). The sharing fellowship of Jesus and his disciples was continued in what Troeltsch called the 'primitive Christian communism of the Book of Acts'.[30] But since then 'there has also been a gradual expropriation of the means of religious production from the Christian people by the clergy' (*CCP*, 112). What had previously belonged to all became available to the many through the privilege of the few. 'Just as there was a social division of labour, an ecclesiastical division of religious labour was introduced' (*CCP*, 113). The control and regulation of the means of religious production was steadily concentrated on fewer and fewer people. They came to possess a monopoly in the supply of the sacraments: 'one group produces the symbolic goods, and another consumes them' (*CCP*, 43). And as a multi-national monopoly the hierarchy also regulated supply from its head office in Rome by conditions of licence which were often stringent and in many respects arbitrary. Continuing with the theory, we see that all relationships and institutions are founded upon this mode of production, and determined by it. The church is necessarily hierarchical, a chain of authority and command. It is necessarily divided into classes, which are defined in relation to production and consumption. Above all authoritarianism, maintenance of the *status quo* and the suppression of dissent are not unfortunate and correctible aberrations, but of the very essence of the institutional church. To give one particular example, which has a certain poignancy in the book, we can consider the Inquisition. According to Boff the Inquisition was little concerned with immorality, but greatly concerned with heresy. The reason is quite clear. Immorality, which leads to confession, penance, absolution and indulgences, actually stimulates activity for religious monopoly capitalism. Sin is good for the religious business. But heresy threatens the acceptance and credibility of the whole system.

On this approach we can therefore see the problem, and the possible solution. The church is not guided by theology, by ideas or ideals. Its nature is determined by its mode of religious production. It is therefore not possible to change the nature of the church or relations within it at the level of ideas, for example by exposing and condemning domination. The church and relations within it, can only be changed when the mode of religious production is replaced. And this is precisely what Boff has experienced in the base communities: 'these communities mean a break with the monopoly of social and religious power and the inauguration of a new religious and social process for restructuring both the church and society, with a different social division of labour as well as an alternative religious division of ecclesiastical labour' (*CCP*, 116). In these communities there is once again a sharing of the religious life. The gifts of the Spirit are not bestowed according to social or religious class. The monopoly is broken and with it the basis of power and consequently the possibility of domination and oppression. The sacramental life is the gift of God to the community and is not the private property of any class. Although Boff presses on, as we have seen, to the more fundamental criticisms, yet the two levels go together. The church is a class society within a class society. It is also characterized by religious capitalism within a capitalist society. Boff has no desire to see the church fragmented, and that is a danger when the Roman church practising religious capitalism within a capitalist society, attempts to impose itself on a church which has broken with religious capitalism. 'Capitalism, as a system of unbalanced social interchange, is an impediment to the universality of the church as long as it only works for the interests of a single class. A democratic and socialist society would seem to offer better objective conditions for a fuller expression of the church's catholicity' (*CCP*, 122).

four

The New Religious Right

In the preceding chapters a pattern has formed in which it would seem that religion has historically failed to condemn and oppose domination through discrimination based on gender, race and class. Indeed in quite specific ways religion has legitimized such domination, both protecting it from attack and providing for it the trappings of moral respectability. Religion has assisted in the furthering of domination carried out by others, and has even participated in domination on its own account. Fortunately the story has not been entirely one-sided. Throughout the same historical periods there have of course been prophetic voices raised in protest, even when institutionalized discrimination continued unabated or subtly changed its grounds and sought re-legitimation. But in each case we have seen how in the present time critical movements have arisen within religious communities to ensure that they should not continue such domination on their own accounts, and if possible that the weight of these communities should be thrown clearly on the side of the oppressed.

The movements we have examined have been for the most part the product of critical thinking from the late 1960s and 1970s. It would be tempting, therefore, to see this too as part of the same pattern, as if historically religion has been on the side of domination, but has now been converted to the side of liberation. The period of the 1960s and 1970s saw the rise of countless good causes, liberal issues and self-criticism among the Western societies. But that period has come to an end. The 1980s have seen a reaction against such a breast-beating confessional ethos. Throughout the world there has been a neo-conservative backlash. Neither in the United Kingdom nor in the United States of America has this been a return to old-style conservatism. As we shall see, neo-conservatism reserves some of its most vitriolic utterances for what it regards as a flabby conservatism which did not have the courage of its convictions, and sought simply to ameliorate the speed at which the older structures and mores of society were dismantled and dismissed. In the USA it is not a return to the former policies of the Republican Party, and in the UK it is very different from that High Toryism so typified by Harold Macmillan, now Lord Stockton. Nothing more tellingly underlined this distinction than his accusation that in implementing a policy of privatization aimed at raising money for tax cuts to the benefit of the already wealthy, Mrs Thatcher was 'selling the family silver'. There spoke the representative of a class which thought it owned the silver, complaining about the tasteless, grasping self-interest of the jumped-up middle class.

What we are observing is not a revival of old-fashioned and to some extent humane conservatism, but a quite new phenomenon, a conservatism which openly sets out to stem and reverse the direction in which society has been moving in recent decades. In neo-conservative circles there is no talk about liberation of the oppressed. While it may not be correct to say that there is an intention to reimpose domination on grounds of gender, race and class, it is certainly true that the thrusting macho ethos of the movement has pointed women back to the home and kitchen sink, has led to the dramatic alienation of black communities, and at least in the UK, has divided the nation more than at any time in the last half-century and revived the rhetoric and the reality of class struggle in a demonstrably unequal society. Centralist, autocratic government is part of the new ethos, and yet it could not proceed unless it was able to tap into latent support at a populist level. The bandwagon is rolling, and those who jump aboard soon pick up the clichés about the poor who want to be poor, the oppressed who prefer things that way, the social casualties who have only themselves to blame. Thus domination is reimposed, but more than that, it is legitimized as a moral duty, for the sake of the health of the country, from which all will eventually benefit. The question is whether in addition to such quasi-Victorian morality, the neo-conservative movement is able to gain religious legitimation. No sooner asked than offered. When the Bishop of Durham in the spring of 1985 pointed to the hardship which government policies were forcing upon the poorest members of the mining communities within his diocese, the Prime Minister was able to greet his considered appeal with the dismissive words that it would not be spring without at least one cuckoo. She could count on ready support within the Church of

England and could afford to push aside unanswered the criticism of the third most senior prelate in the established church.

It would seem, therefore, that although the pattern so far has been of religion on the side of domination, giving way to religion on the side of liberation, it does not represent a permanent shift of position. There are many powerful religious voices basically in agreement with the neo-conservative movement. We must recognize that now the New Right has succeeded in occupying the high moral ground. It has now become the *status quo* against which progressive voices must argue. The liberation case can no longer assume that it has right on its side. It has to begin again. Nor can it take for granted the support of religion. The New Religious Right is already legitimizing neo-conservative values and identifying the ethos of that movement as the will of God for our time. It is salutary to observe that the New Religious Right has appeared not only in the UK, formerly a progressive and liberal country, but also in the two other areas which we have studied in some detail, the USA and Latin America. In this chapter I can illustrate how the New Religious Right lends its support to movements which intensify domination, and on occasion contributes to domination on its own account.

Several years ago I attended an international conference. One of the speakers was a German bishop. I can still remember the excitement I felt in listening to his lecture, an excitement which I imagine must have been experienced by marine biologists when they discovered that the coelocanth was not after all extinct. The learned bishop actually held those doctrines in their traditional form which I had thought no longer possible in twentieth-century Europe. It was with something of the same fascination that I read the recent work of the Brazilian Presbyterian theologian Rubem Alves, entitled *Protestantism and Repression* (= *PR*).[1] He describes a theological position which I thought could no longer be found anywhere in the world. In the late 1960s Alves was one of the first of the new generation of Latin American theologians to attract attention in the Western world. *A Theology of Human Hope* was followed by *Tomorrow's Child*,[2] and the books established his reputation as an exciting inter-disciplinary thinker with something valuable to say in Latin America from which theologians of other countries could benefit. Even at that time the Presbyterian Church in Brazil, to which Alves belonged, still maintained its original character, as a democratic movement with a liberal policy on education, and committed to the secular goal of separation of church and state. It was progressive, too, in social, economic and political matters, working for the transformation of the country, and denouncing the domination of the country by the then reactionary Catholic church. The Catholic church in turn saw the Presbyterian influence as subversive and giving aid, intentionally or unintentionally, to the Communists. However, with a surprising role reversal, the post-Vatican II Catholic Church has become progressive in social and economic matters and critical of political abuse and injustice, while at the same time the Presbyterian church has reimposed control and discipline over those who have sought to become involved or involve the church in such matters. The sub-title of Alves' book is 'A Brazilian Case Study', but in fact the position which he describes is not peculiar to Brazil. The study is not a microscope, but a mirror. With great care and subtlety Alves describes a movement, a mechanism and a mind-set which is present everywhere in the Western world. Richard Shaull, an American theologian who has spent many years in Latin America, has written a Foreword, in which he comments on the transformation in the life of the church. 'The Presbyterian Church, rather than sustaining this quality of life, is identified with the most reactionary political developments and does its part to legitimize a repressive order' (*PR*, xi). We might assume that in Latin America domination has given way to liberation, not least in Christian circles, but here is a counter-movement in which liberation is deliberately set aside and domination reimposed through religion. If we note its characteristics in Latin America we shall be well equipped to recognize the same forces at work in the USA and in the UK.

In the preceding chapters we have been considering various socially constructed views of reality. There are social constructions which tend to legitimize things as they are and other social constructions which prophetically challenge what is with the moral imperatives of what should be. Theological statements are also social constructions, and they have an immediate effect on the social and political as well as the religious lives of individuals and communities. Alves is drawing attention to a theological position which, even while it seems unconcerned with the socio-political, has important long-term implications for those within the church and also by consequence those outside. He is about to describe a theological position, but begins with a summary of the main characteristics of this brand of Brazilian Protestantism. It is resistant to innovation. 'This resistance is given legitimacy by sacralizing forms of thinking and acting which have been inherited from the past' (*PR*, xxi). But the implications have practical consequences not only for the interpretation of the past, but for present-day life. 'It finds expression in the legitimation of the existing setup of power and authority, and in the absence of prophetic criticism' (*PR*, xxi). Precisely as it disclaims any interest in the socio-political, it relates directly to this sphere. As in the case of all ideologies of domination, the socially constructed view not only comes to seem both natural and true, but is fervently supported by those who benefit least from it and suffer most under it. Alves quotes Alvin Gouldner with approval. 'The old society is not held together merely by force and violence, or expedience and prudence. The old society maintains itself also through theories and ideologies that establish its hegemony over the minds of men, who therefore do not merely bite their tongues but submit to it willingly' (quoted *PR*, xxxiii). Alves therefore sets out to give an account not merely of a theological position, but of a religious ideology with very important and direct consequences for the people of Brazil. Since the same new Protestant spirit is not peculiar to Brazil but is found throughout the world, his analysis has unfortunately much wider application.

Alves refers to the phenomenon as Right Doctrine Protestantism, abbreviating it to RDP. He focuses on its central feature. 'The fact that it stresses agreement with a series of doctrinal affirmations, which are regarded as expressions of the truth and which must be affirmed without any shadow of doubt, as the precondition for participation in the ecclesial community' (*PR*, 8). To enter RDP it is necessary to be converted, but the *metanoia*, the change of understanding, is of a very particular order. Although the conversion is of the individual, the state achieved is not unique or peculiar to the individual. Rather, the new consciousness is already precisely defined by RDP. 'To be saved, the individuals must adjust their consciousness completely to that of the community. The collective consciousness is a sacred absolute. The evidence of individuals' salvation is their spoken *repetition* of the community's knowledge' (*PR*, 86). RDP has the marks of an ideology, a closed system which already encapsulates the truth, which neither anticipates nor needs to learn anything from the present or the future. Converts do not begin upon a quest or pilgrimage of faith and doubt. They inherit a highly rational world view from which the contradictions of actual experience are eliminated as if they were heresies. Alves sets out a long quotation from Lezek Kolakowski almost as a motto for the book, in which the Polish philosopher concludes, 'total consistency is tantamount in practice to fanaticism, while inconsistency is the source of tolerance' (quoted (*PR*, v). In this closed system, Alves tells us, 'faith is transformed into dogma' (*PR*, 50). This is not surprising, since one of the characteristics of an ideology is that it has already established absolute truth and knowledge and proves incorrigible in the face of actual experience. If the facts do not fit, so much the worse for the facts. But more, it encourages those who live within it to discount the values of their own experience over against that of the community. In *The German Ideology* Marx warned that 'Life is not determined by consciousness, but consciousness by life'.[3] Our understanding should derive from our experience rather than from a pre-established dogmatic picture. Alves echoes this view as he describes the outlook of the convert to RDP. 'My absolute knowledge *prohibits* the real from surprising me, from revealing itself differently. Experience is not the criterion of my thinking; my thinking is the criterion of any and all possible experience' (*PR*, 55). Thus for RDP the Bible is a surprise-free book. No new word will be heard, certainly nothing which will call in question the dogmatic picture of how things are. This is a most un-biblical approach to the Bible when compared to the words of Jesus, 'I have yet many things to say to you, but you cannot bear them now' (John 16.12). Even Paul confessed, 'Now I know in part . . .' (I Cor. 13.12). The trouble with Right Doctrine Protestantism is that it does not see through a glass darkly.

If converts are required to accept an already existing account of reality, they are also given direction about the nature of evil in the world. Since it would undermine the authority of those who maintain the absolute world-view if they were thought capable of sin, converts learn that evil and corruption refer neither to institutions nor dispositions but to specific forms of individual behaviour. Alves draws up a list of those sins which are of most concern to RDP: sexual sins, violations of Sunday, smoking, drinking, gambling, crimes against property, theft, dishonesty, crimes against thought, i.e. heresy. Those who abstain from and avoid such sins live lives of holiness. Thus morality is a matter of conduct, rather than conscience, and church discipline 'is ruled by the logic of justification by works' (*PR*, 139). But are these central religious concerns not somehow familiar? Have we not met them in the Gospels? According to Alves, they were the primary concerns of those religious purists who opposed Jesus. 'The Protestant morality of debits and credits has a moral logic that is the opposite of Jesus' moral logic' (*PR*, 151). And this leads us to a crucial matter, the RDP's lack of response to the social teaching of Jesus. I am not referring here to our common failing to do as much as we could for the orphan, the widow and the immigrant, to show love and concern for our neighbour. There is something more fundamental at stake here, and more sinister. The failure of RDP to respond to the social teaching of Jesus does not arise out of sloth but is a consequence of its ideological view of things. All that is necessary for salvation has already been achieved in the past. God has already conquered in Christ. What is, is in the providence of God. 'That is why the mark of salvation is not action but absolute knowledge, why Protestants give priority to the indicative mood over the imperative. The indicative describes things as they are' (*PR*, 94). This approach goes back to what has already been said about the Bible; 'Texts in the indicative mood must be interpreted literally; texts in the imperative mood do not have to be interpreted literally (*PR*, 76). In this preference RDP is revealed as ideology rather than biblical religion. The convert who drinks alcohol does not threaten RDP, and in repenting actually confirms its position. But a convert who does not believe what is required, including presumably that Jonah was swallowed by a whale and survived, threatens the whole basis of absolute knowledge. 'I don't know of any instances where ethics has provoked a crisis in the Brazilian Church. But it is fatal to challenge the literal veracity of texts in the indicative mood, texts which tell us how things were' (*PR*, 76). Here is the primacy of knowledge over morality, wisdom over goodness, doctrine over life. Converts who do wrong are still within the community: those who do not believe everything must be thrust out, for they are a threat to the whole institution. Inadvertently the convert might express doubt on some matter of fact. With that the original welcome turns to rejection. 'The certainty of truth is the smiling face of intolerance' (*PR*, 83). The attitude towards the Bible concerns the *is* rather than the *ought*, and this attitude is carried forward into social life generally. Christ has already died for the sins of the world. The answer to the crisis of the modern world is the same answer to all generations and all situations. People must come to understand what really is the case, to believe what is the truth. Through understanding and right belief, the problems of the world will be solved. 'A social ethic has no essential place in the RDP universe. A Protestant believer could say everything that ought to be said without once alluding to the necessity of transforming the world' (*PR*, 152). Since Alves is writing in the first instance about the situation in Brazil, it is instructive to look at the place of the poor in RDP espeically, since this was a central feature of the work of Sobrino and the Brazilian Leonardo Boff which we examined in the previous chapter. According to liberation theology, Jesus speaks different words to the rich and the poor: words of challenge and judgment to the rich, words of comfort and blessing to the poor. How people relate to the poor becomes a test of how they relate to God. Not so for RDP. Since there is but one truth, everyone receives the same message regardless. 'Our conclusion, then, is that poverty is not a basic problem for this brand of Protestantism. It does not really matter that a person is poor. What is of crucial importance is the subjective way in which he or she lives this poverty. The proper attitudes are resignation, patient submission, gratitude, and the certainty that all things work together for the good of those who love God' (*PR*, 156–7). But is this biblical religion, or simply ideology? Paul, in the midst of trials and tribulations, a man who daily suffered for his obedience to his calling as a Christian apostle, can utter a profound truth. 'And we know that all things work together for good to them that love God . . .' (Rom. 8.28). It is one thing for one who suffers to so confess this faith. It is quite another for those who are not suffering to lay this assurance on the poor and oppressed. Then profound religious faith becomes the legitimation of the self-interest of the ruling class. As Alves puts it, in such circumstances talk of providence 'becomes a justification of reality as fatal necessity; it absolutizes things as they are. Facts are transformed into values. This rules out ethical talk as to whether something should or should not be' (*PR*, 99). Alves, in a thought which has resonances with Bonhoeffer's prison letters, therefore reflects that instead of exposing poverty and condemning it, RDP sees in suffering the opportunity to evangelize. Nothing could better illustrate or justify the righteous indignation of Marx's accusation that religion is the 'opium of the people'.[4] Except that we should identify the suppliers and pushers as the RDP, who do not themselves require such aids. And while I mention Marx, we should notice the perceptive conclusion to which Alves comes. In the previous chapter we saw that Sobrino characterized Latin American theology as belonging to the tradition of Marx, taking as its motto the XIth Thesis on Feuerbach: 'The philosophers have only interpreted the world in various ways; the point is to change it.' But RDP promotes the indicative above the imperative, knowledge above action, understanding above obedience. What is, is in the Providence of God. Therefore there is a religious duty *not* to interfere. 'The problem is not to transform reality because it has already been transformed, reconciled, and made new in Christ. What we have to do is transform our way of feeling and perceiving it. Thus we could formulate the viewpoint of this sort of Protestantism as a reversal of Marx's eleventh thesis on Feuerbach: "Human beings have tried in various ways to transform the world; the point is not to transform the world but to reinterpret it"' (*PR*, 42). There is no need in RDP to transform the world, but to understand it. To become a Christian is to believe and accept what is: there is no obligation to become involved in social transformation, either through action or intercession. Alves concludes laconically, 'I see prayer as a Freudian slip in the RDP world' (*PR*, 113). I noted in the last chapter that to be even-handed in a class society is to favour those who control how things are. RDP, even while eschewing political involvement, therefore legitimizes the *status quo*. Alves is able to quote an official statement which, after Paul's advice in Romans 13, advocates that Christians submit to the authorities, for they are ordained of God. And that at a time when a military junta had ousted the democratic government.

Lest we lose sight of the wood for the trees, we have been examining the case of the Presbyterian church in Brazil, as a specific instance of a neo-conservative religious movement which has the effect of bestowing religious legitimation on neo-conservative elements in the ruling class. Ironically, the fact that they claim to have no such intention only succeeds in guaranteeing the outcome. This kind of religion does not seek to identify, expose and condemn forms of domination within society. By its lack of social ethics it allows domination to continue unchallenged. By sacralizing what is, it inadvertently confers legitimation on these relationships. And worst of all, it contributes to domination on its own account, seeing suffering as an opportunity of evangelism rather than an occasion of solidarity.

Before leaving RDP we might note the depressing parallel between the experiences of Alves and Boff. The further irony is that pre-conciliar Catholicism and the RDP see themselves as occupying positions at the extreme end of a spectrum from each other. And yet if we take the circular model of extremism rather than a linear one, we should not be surprised to find that both institutions share certain common characteristics, especially in the way in which they treat progressive theologians. Erasmo Braga, another Brazilian Protestant, has commented on the same situation. In Brazil, 'Protestantism is a negative image of Catholicism, with all the inconveniences of a negative' (quoted *PR*, 167). RDP, in other words, is defined negatively by its image of Catholicism. But the way in which it operates bears a striking resemblance. Alves refers to the matter of biblical hermeneutics, which as we have seen is an important issue for RDP. 'The *magisterium* of the Catholic Church and the *confessions* of the Protestant Churches perform exactly the same function . . .' (*PR*, 71). And the astonishing conclusion that in this area, 'What, then, separates Protestants from Catholics? Nothing, absolutely nothing' (*PR*, 71). In the last chapter we noted that Boff claimed that the Inquisition was not interested in immorality, only in heresy. We have seen that the RDP is likewise less concerned with right action than with right belief. 'The Inquisition, for example, did not punish people who committed moral faults. Robbery, adultery, and murder were matters for the secular courts. The Inquisition was concerned with the much more serious crimes against orthodox thinking' (*PR*, 196). Thus RDP, like pre-conciliar Catholicism, imposes in addition to all forms of secular domination a further domination of its own members. There is a final point which might be made in this context. RDP does not take into account any changes taking place within the Catholic Church. The reason is that its own identity and *raison d'être* are bound up with opposing old-style Catholicism. It has a stake in maintaining that nothing has changed and that change is not possible. Otherwise RDP itself might have to change. And as we have seen, it is built upon the claim that it already possesses absolute truth. To admit change in the Catholic church would be to sow the seeds of its own redundancy and destruction. Anyone familiar with the situation in Northern Ireland will see the relevance of Alves' analysis.

Before we turn to consider the situation in the United Kingdom, however, we must consider the development of neo-conservatism in the USA. Richard Shaull in his Foreword claims that Alves' book speaks to America. 'For we are surrounded by abundant evidence that confirms this thesis. I would mention only the alliance of right-wing political leaders and evangelical preachers and movements in attempts to defeat liberal congressmen, in opposition to the Equal Rights Amendment, in movements to "defend the family" and "expose its enemies", in efforts to justify more military spending and revive the rhetoric of the Cold War' (*PR*, xvi). All of these elements are found in what is called the New Religious Right in America. One of its main features is the opposition to liberation movements leading to the reimposition of domination in its several forms.

The United States is a country which British people should understand better than most. It is not simply the fact that we are two nations divided by a common language; many British people have lived and worked in America for varying lengths of time before returning home. Many more have spent extended vacations there, and even more have welcomed relations from America who come seeking their roots and Harrods' credit facilities. But apart from or in addition to all of these personal connections, it sometimes seems as though at least a third of all TV programmes shown in Britain have been imported from the USA. Through this medium we are familiarized with the American way of life – i.e. with organized crime, a nomadic population, temporary marriages, high-speed car chases ending in multiple mayhem, and a glimpse into that exclusive world of tasteless luxury and crass materialism into which we should all like to be drawn by accident. But there is one element of American life which profoundly distinguishes it from life in Britain or the European democracies at large. G. K. Chesterton perceptively identified it when, commenting on a visit there in 1921, he described America as 'a nation with the soul of a church'.[5] Churchgoing is much higher there than here, but that is not the decisive difference. It has to do with the history of the country and above all with a religious perception of America as the new Promised Land, a land in which God could begin again with a people who would be faithful to him. If they kept their side of the covenant, then they would be rewarded by America, the richest and most powerful country in the history of the world. Clearly something has gone wrong. For the last twenty years there has been a crisis in American life. Different countries interpret crises in different ways. It has been said that the difference between crises in Britain and Ireland is that in Britain things are always serious, but never desperate, while in Ireland, things are always desperate but never serious. But when we turn to the crisis in American life, many interpret it in the light of this religious perception of the manifest destiny of America. Political turmoil is taken as a symptom of a deeper religious malaise. It is not at all surprising, therefore, to hear these sentiments expressed by the Rev Jerry Falwell. 'But I do not believe that America will be turned around solely by working in the areas of politics, economics and defense, as important as these may be. These are crucial issues that face us in the 1980s, but America can only be turned around as her people make godly, moral choices. When history records these ten years, I think it will be fair to project that this will have probably been, since the days of the American Revolution, the most important decade this nation has known.'[6] Jerry Falwell is looking for a religious revival, a return to the old faith, to the tap roots of America. The Great Awakening led up to the Revolutionary War and the founding of the Republic. A century later in the period of reconstruction after the Civil War there were the early signs of the Second Great Awakening. And now as America, keeper of the peace in the Cold War, enters the third century of the Republic, it is appropriate for a new religious revival to recall the nation to its destiny and the values which made it great. But is the current revival a religious revival? Or rather, does it recall America to its biblical faith and are the values promoted by this revival biblical values at all?

Few Americans today share the faith of the English Puritans who set up the early colonies three centuries ago. It is unlikely that there could be a revival of this ascetic and disciplined religion. But Puritanism has been long since overtaken by another religious tradition, one which specifically distinguished itself from Christianity, civil religion. There is evidence that the revival in America in the last decade has been a revival of civil religion rather than evangelical Christianity.

Although America today is a politically conservative country, its founders were much influenced by the radical, even revolutionary leaders of the European Enlightenment. Those who were responsible for the drawing up of a new constitution suitable for democratic government by consent read with interest Jean Jacques Rousseau's treatise on *The Social Contract* (= *SC*), published only fourteen years before the Declaration of Independence. Throughout history a fundamental problem has been faced by the leaders of new states which have no tribal or national identity, the problem of unification. It was solved for Alexander the Great in the fourth century BC by the creation of a new imperial cult, centred on his person. Perhaps surprisingly, in facing the same problem of the unification of a people Rousseau also turns to religion. It was very different in content, but very similar in function. The nation would not be unified by the abolition of religion: 'no state has ever been founded without a religious basis . . .'[7] But positive or historic religions will not perform the unifying function which Rousseau had in mind. They cause divisions, and in the case of Christianity it is always possible that at some point it will be found necessary to obey God rather than men. Rousseau therefore proposes a non-contentious form of religion which will be a source of agreement rather than discord. 'There is therefore a purely civil profession of faith of which the Sovereign should fix the articles, not exactly as religious dogmas, but as social sentiments without which a man cannot be a good citizen or a faithful subject' (*SC*, 276). What he has in mind is the channelling of religious sentiments towards the state. Members of society are to apply the devotion associated with religion to this new subject. The people will be unified through the expression of these religious sentiments and devotion to the new state. Religion will not divide them from each other or from the state but, as its etymology implies, religion will be a force which binds people together. Of course even a civil religion must have some content, and Rousseau proposed a brief list of notions on which he thought most people would agree without difficulty. 'The dogmas of civil religion ought to be few, simple, and exactly worded, without explanation or commentary. The existence of a mighty, intelligent, and beneficent divinity, possessed of foresight and providence, the life to come, the happiness of the just, the punishment of the wicked, the sanctity of the social contract and the laws: these are its positive dogmas' (*SC*, 276).

This Enlightenment deism is not Christianity. It is natural religion but with a family resemblance to central elements in Old Testament theism. There is nothing in it offensive to Christians of whatever denomination. Indeed it could be affirmed by adherents of many religions. More to the point, it could even be accepted in its vagueness by many who adhere to no religion at all. This was what Rousseau intended and this was what happened in America. It enabled political leaders to rally support and unite the nation on the basis of religious sentiments and a general religious perspective on the development of the nation. Thus Thomas Jefferson in his Second Inaugural Address, in 1805, could speak as a deist but be heard by Christians as if he were a Christian, yet without offending or alienating those who were indifferent to the Christian religion. 'I shall need, too, the favor of that Being in whose hands we are, who led our fathers, as Israel of old, from their native land and planted them in a country flowing with all the necessary comforts of life . . .'[8] The twentieth century saw both the decline in the original evangelical faith, and a massive influx of immigrants who never shared it. But in the tradition of civil religion, they were baptized into their new life by the Pledge of Allegiance, this credal statement which Americanizes them as believers. Nor is this a purely abstract notion. This civil religion has its shrine in the Mall in Washington. Those who enter the National Archives find that if they speak they do so in hushed tones. As they fall in line to shuffle round the high vaulted apse-like hall they peer into glass cases which display holy relics. At last if only for a few moments they are allowed to gaze upon the central displays, lifting children up to see, so that they might be better people. Before them, more like parchment than tablets of stone, lie the holy texts, the Declaration of Independence and the Constitution. But civil religion could not exist with a distant shrine only, and in schools throughout the land children turn to the religious symbol of the flag before beginning the calling of the day. There is a liturgical year, rounded out by

Thanksgiving, Memorial Day and the Fourth of July, Independence Day. If in the Pledge they confess their faith in 'one nation under God', so perhaps fittingly for the devotees of capitalism it is on the coins of the land that all are daily reminded 'In God we Trust'. There has undoubtedly been a religious revival in America in the last decade, less of evangelical Christian religion than of the civil religion of American nationalism. We must now examine the path by which Old Time Religion has been infiltrated by the New Religious Right.

Conservatives are often regarded as cautious, reactionary and suspicious of innovation. The world as it was suited them very well, and they wish to conserve it from substantial change. Nothing could be further from the reality of the New Right in America, typified by Richard Viguerie. The Viguerie Company, of Falls Church, Virginia, is one of the largest private direct mailing companies in the world. Its strength is not that it has a vast list of names and addresses, but that the list has been selectively built up over a period of twenty years. Those on the list are likely to be susceptible to the subject of any particular mail shot, sympathetic to the causes and issues defined by the New Right. The resources of the Viguerie Company are made available on the basis of an ideological test. About fifteen per cent of its clients are political candidates seeking election or re-election. They would of course be politically conservative, as are most of the organizations for which Viguerie agrees to work. As he says in his book *The New Right* (= *NR*), 'Our clients are concerned with issues such as gun control, pro-life, prayer in school, abuses by national union officials, wasteful government spending, high taxes, immorality on TV and in the movies, an educational system that can't educate, national defense and many other issues'[9] To choose one example, the decision about the Panama Canal Treaty in 1978 illustrates the new approach. The New Right formed a coalition of some twenty national organizations on the issue, but more significantly carried the argument past the political parties directly to the people. The Conservative Caucus mailed three million letters, The American Security Council mailed two million, The American Conservative Union mailed out two million letters, while the 'Truth Squad', consisting of several conservative senators and congressmen, reached an estimated ten million Americans through TV and newspaper coverage. At the same time very large amounts of money were being raised for the cause. Viguerie claimed with some justification that this whole experience 'was one more proof of the reduced importance of political parties. And of the New Right's ability to engage in and finance important political activity outside a major political party' (*NR*, 69). The New Right spent over three million dollars. They lost the vote, but gained immensely. They became more experienced in the new form of political campaigning, in the run-up to their main target – the 1980 presidential election. And incidentally, Viguerie added a further 400,000 new names to his list.

The New Right as exemplified by Viguerie is not reactionary or Luddite. It has made use of the latest technology to create a new form of political action. It is estimated that the New Right is in this matter a decade ahead of the opposition. Viguerie's involvement in direct mailing came about almost by chance. He was born in Texas in 1933, and his early heroes were Douglas MacArthur and Joseph McCarthy. His first political experience was working within the Republican Party for Eisenhower, in 1952 and 1956. In 1961 he went to New York to work for Young Americans for Freedom. The organization, less than a year old, was almost bankrupt and Viguerie began visiting prominent political and business people to solicit money. He found this a strain, being shy by temperament, and decided to write instead. From this humble start, the direct mailing empire grew. The next year he moved to Washington and in 1964 set up his own direct mail company on Capitol Hill. The company was to serve Viguerie's political cause, but the cause was not identified with a party. He was prepared to support one Republican against another in primaries, on the basis of conservative sympathies. He would not work on behalf of the Democrat George McGovern because of his liberal position. But neither would he work for Richard Nixon who, though a Republican, was turning towards Keynesian economics and the development of a welfare programme. Yet Viguerie was prepared to work on behalf of George Wallace, who though a Democrat was sound on about eighty per cent of conservative issues.

The New Right is therefore an ideological movement with distinct values and a clear approach to contemporary issues. It is quite different from a broad consensus political party. It is also populist, reaching over the heads of party leaders to address voters and potential contributors directly in their homes. The father figures of the New Right were William F. Buckley Jr and Barry Goldwater. Buckley has been for over thirty years a brilliant advocate of the conservative case. He was the founder of Young Americans for Freedom and is one of the few conservative intellectuals to display a fine sense of humour in debate. It was Barry Goldwater who in the 1964 presidential election gave national exposure to what was to become the agenda of the New Right. He was defeated at the polls, but achieved his goal of offering to the American people 'a choice, not an echo'. It was he who claimed to speak for millions of 'silent Americans' who constitute the majority. Viguerie mentions other conservatives who stand in this significant New Right tradition, including Ronald Reagan and Milton Friedman. When in 1974 Gerald Ford chose the liberal Nelson Rockefeller as vice-president, the New Right knew that they could not rely on a party, but must become leaders themselves of the new movement. By 1977 it was nationally reported, 'A third force is quietly building a political apparatus that pointedly disregards party labels.'[10] It was this third force which threw itself behind Ronald Reagan in the 1980 presidential election, and at the same time targeted liberal senators for defeat. 'The voters of Idaho and South Dakota finally got to know the *real* Frank Church and the *real* George McGovern – the ones Fidel Castro knows. Because conservatives have mastered the new technology, we've been able to bypass the Left's near-monopoly of the national news media' (*NR*, 6). In the euphoria of 1980 the New Right believed that they were largely responsible for the conservative victory, that in future they would be able to make and break candidates through new-style political action. They believed that America was basically a conservative country, but that people were inhibited from speaking out and identifying their real position. When we recall that our examination of the New Right is to enquire into the question whether the movement turns back from liberation in gender, race and class towards domination, Viguerie's reading of the situation is instructive. 'They may care very little about things the liberals feel strongly about, like the Equal Rights Amendment. They may hide their real feelings and give the answers they think pollsters expect, because they think it's "unenlightened", or "bad taste", or may be seen as a sign of a "lack of compassion" to give non-liberal answers' (*NR*, 181). And it is of some significance that our three issues are prominent in Viguerie's characterization of the liberalism which he opposes. 'To liberals, civil rights has come to mean not equality of opportunity but reverse racism and forced busing. Women's rights has come to mean denial of the first right of all human beings, regardless of sex: the right to life. Civil liberties has come to mean not the free exercise of religion but forbidding school children a daily moment of voluntary prayer. Compassion for the poor has come to mean contempt for the middle class' (*NR*, 18).

Finally, there is another important strand in the development of the New Right, the enlisting of the support of conservative Christians. There is the assumption that people who are conservative in religion will be conservative on the other matters constituting the agenda of the New Right. Thus Viguerie quotes with approval the words of the young New Right leader George Gilder. 'The fact is, however, that capitalism thrives on religious faith and decays without it. Capitalist progress is based on the acceptance of risks that cannot be demonstrated to pay off in any one lifetime. Thus, it relies on faith in the future, and in Providence' (quoted *NR*, 20). In an Epilogue Viguerie chides President Reagan for accepting the support of the conservative religious leaders before his election but refusing to see them once settled into the White House. 'America needs a rebirth of religious commitment. I urge you to use your great skills as a communicator and regularly ask people to seek the solution to our personal and national problems in God' (*NR*, 190). Apparently the Great Communicator speaks but does not listen. Yet Viguerie specifically set out to recruit religious leaders to assist the New Right, not least because the tele-evengelists already had their own networks and audiences who were likely to be receptive to the message of the movement. Indeed this is precisely the point. To what extent was there a blurring of conservative religion with conservative politics? To what extent were people led to believe that support for one was support for the other? Pollster Lou Harris calculated that Reagan owed two-thirds of his victory margin to evangelical Christians, who switched their support from the born-again but liberal Jimmy Carter, to the not-so-clearly born-again but conservative Ronald Reagan (*NR*, 178). If conservative evangelical Christians were led to believe that the values of the New Right were Christian values, and that the agenda of the New Right would lead America back to the covenant with God, then this was due in large measure to the alliance of tele-evangelists and the New Right. No one epitomizes this identification more clearly than the Rev Jerry Falwell, who wrote an Introduction to Viguerie's book. In this he provides a religious legitimation for the values and policies of the New Right, a movement which as we have seen was committed to turn back the wave of liberation which threatened to transform Western society.

Falwell begins his Introduction by rejecting recent trends within American society. 'In the last several years, Americans have literally stood by and watched as godless, spineless leaders have brought our nation floundering to the brink of death.' As he sees it, America is as a result a country 'depraved, decadent and demoralized'. While most people would recognize that good and evil exist in an imperfect world, Falwell reverts to what in political theory is termed Manichaeism, the identification of good and evil with social groups. This is a dangerous,

pretentious and self-congratulatory division of the world, a demoniz-
ation of some people as if they were the source of all evil. But of
particular interest here is the fact that this evangelist is allowing the New
Right to draw the line in the moral division of the world. In the following
lengthy quotation Falwell uncritically accepts Viguerie's two groups as
identical with the god-fearing and the god-less.

> Mr Viguerie has not detailed a new group; he has described the
> backbone of our country – those citizens who are pro-family, pro-
> moral, pro-life, and pro-American, who have integrity and believe in
> hard work, those who pledge allegiance to the flag and proudly sing
> our national anthem. He has described that group of citizens who love
> their country and are willing to sacrifice for her. America was built on
> faith in God, on integrity, and on hard work. Mr Viguerie clearly
> names those who have not been committed to those principles, and
> have thus led to the weakening and the humiliation of a once great
> America.

This statement sums up the relationship of the New Religious Right to
the New Right itself. The New Religious Right takes over uncritically
the values and the agenda of the New Right. Its only contribution is a
religious legitimation by which neo-conservatist ideology is pronounced
identical with the will of God for America, by which too those who in
recent years have sought to end domination and oppression are
condemned as the exponents of 'godless, liberal philosophies'. Rousseau wished to avoid the inevitable prophetic critical judgments of
biblical Christianity. He advocated a civil religion which would serve
nationalism. We shall now have to consider whether the New Religious
Right is not simply an example of civil religion, tricked out with the
language and proof texts of biblical religion, but delivering as required a
religious devotion to American nationalism.

As we have seen, Falwell considers that the crisis in American life is a
religious crisis. Later he has a good deal to say about the moral
dimensions of this crisis, but it is also evident in other areas. The first,
and it is therefore obviously of prime importance, is that for the first time
in modern times America may not be the most powerful military country
in the world. This has come about not through lack of resources, but
through lack of will. As he points out in *Listen America!* (= *LA*), 'We are
not committed to victory. We are not committed to greatness' (*LA*, 9).
This could hardly be the first symptom of crisis for biblical religion, but
of course it must be of paramount importance to the religion of

American nationalism. The second symptom of crisis in American society is welfarism. Government is taking money in taxation and giving it to the poor. And that, it would seem, is a crisis. Looked at more closely, the crisis is not in charity. Falwell advocates charity if undertaken by religious bodies or private organizations. The crisis must therefore be that by its intervention the federal government is changing economic relationships within society. Which is another way of saying that the threat is to capitalism. Falwell offers a spirited, though ill-supported, religious defence of capitalism. 'The free-enterprise system is clearly outlined in the Book of Proverbs in the Bible. Jesus Christ made it clear that the work ethic was part of His plan for man. Ownership of property is biblical. Competition in business is biblical. Ambitious and successful business managment is clearly outlined as a part of God's plan for His people' (*LA*, 12). What is at stake is apparently the ethos of the country. Is it to be a country in which the poor are cared for by right, with all the fiscal and structural ramifications involved? Or is it a country which is geared to enabling those who can get on to do so at the expense of the poor? Robert Bellah describes this pole of American culture as 'utilitarian individualism'.[11] While, as we saw in the last chapter, God has a particular concern for the poor, Falwell has a particular concern for capitalism. Once again, his roots would seem to lie in civil rather than biblical religion. When we come to discuss the case of the UK this will be an important issue, since it is the objective of Thatcherite neo-conservatism to defeat the ethos of a welfare state and replace it with the ethos of self-help and enterprise. There is, however, a third ingredient in the religious crisis of American life, namely leadership. Many would agree with this point. For those of us who have a real affection for America it is one of the most disappointing features of public life there that at every level there is evidence of corruption, from dog-catcher to the White House. When a friend visiting my family from a small town where we once lived brought us up to date with the news, it included the fact that the mayor was under investigation and the sheriff was already in jail. Yes, it must be counted as an open wound in the American body politic. Yet this is not really what Falwell has in mind. He is concerned that leaders do not lead, at least not in the direction which he favours. He is concerned that contrary to Romans 13, a significant number of people do not give automatic support to political institutions. After Watergate we might think that this is to the moral credit of such people, but Falwell obviously does not want a slackening of social control. 'The authority, "the higher powers" – the President, the Congress, the judiciary – are ordained of God' (*LA*, 14). A further aspect of the crisis is that leadership should be male leadership. This is being undermined in various ways. The position of the husband and father is being eroded. The male leadership of the churches is likewise weakened. 'We must stand against the Equal Rights Amendment, the feminist revolution, and the homosexual revolution' (*LA*, 17). This would seem to be an attempt to turn the clock back on the feminist movement, the movement to end domination on the grounds of gender. Falwell claims that the Equal Rights Amendment is a violation of Ephesians 5.23, 'For the husband is the head of the wife as Christ is the head of the church . . .' This snatching at a text avoids the more complex attempt to discover what is the biblical teaching on the relations between men and women in Christ, as discussed in Chapter 1. Another typical ploy is the demonizing of feminists. He tells us that 'Most of the women who are leaders in the feminist movement promote an immoral life style' (*LA*, 106). As we have seen, leadership based on such domination is not the only or highest expression of biblical religion. It is, however, in keeping with a certain macho image of nationalism. These three examples of a religious crisis do not reflect priorities in biblical religion. Where do they come from and why are they given such a prominent position? They are typical of the concerns of the New Right. Indeed, Viguerie has chapters on 'Our Primary Goal: Military Supremacy'; 'The Tax-revolt' and 'The Pro-Family Movement'. The fact that these concerns appear in a book written by an evangelical preacher does not make them biblical, but it does lend them a powerful and valuable religious legitimation, particularly among those who are not capable of distinguishing between the two positions.

We have noted that in his introduction to Viguerie's book Falwell allows the New Right to define the god-fearing and the god-less. He takes over the main concerns of the New Right in describing the religious crisis in American life. I can mention a third example of the influence of the New Right in Falwell's work. Since I have been describing Falwell's position as essentially the civil religion of American nationalism, it is of some significance that less than three weeks before the 1980 Presidential election he issued a 'Christian Bill of Rights'. This was in the form of ten Amendments, thus recalling the original number of amendments passed by the Congress in 1789. These amendments, the Bill of Rights, were to reassure those who 'feared that centralization of power would encroach mightily on their individual liberties'.[12] It may seem sacrilegious to Americans to refer at this point to an article by

Marx which is relevant here. In 1843 Marx wrote two essays 'On the Jewish Question' in response to issues raised by Bruno Bauer. As ever he broadened the implications beyond the subject as it had been understood up till then. Marx chose to illustrate by reference to the constitutional separation of church and state in America. He saw American society divided between 'the general interest and private interest, the schism between the political state and civil society . . .' (*Works* 3, 155). Two different forms of existence are set before man: 'life in the political community, in which he considers himself a communal being, and life in civil society, in which he acts as a private individual, regards other men as a means, degrades himself into a means, and becomes the plaything of alien powers. The relation of the political state to civil society is just as spiritual as the relation of heaven to earth' (*Works* 3, 154). The distinction which Marx is making is between man's true life, his social being, which is enabled because his membership in society, and man's alienated life, his individual existence over against society. The Bill of Rights, by concentrating on individual liberties, encouraged man to see himself standing over against society. 'None of the so-called rights of man, therefore, go beyond egoistic man, beyond man as a member of civil society, that is, an individual withdrawn into himself, into the confines of his private interests and private caprice, and separated from the community' (*Works* 3, 164). If the Constitution lays the foundation for a new community, the Bill of Rights attempts to preserve the life of the individual as if he lived in a merely civil society. The New Right has of course emphasized the rights of man over against the community. In drawing up a 'Christian Bill of Rights' Falwell is providing religious legitimation for this view that the greatest danger of American society is the erosion of freedom to pursue utilitarian individualism.

The actual 'Amendments' are a rag-bag of issues typical of the agenda of the New Religious Right: anti-abortion, self-reliance, anti-euthanasia, support for the state, prayer in schools, private Christian schools, Christian moral influence in public life, moral and military strength, traditional family. In each case the biblical reference to a proof text is given, probably on the assumption that no one will take the trouble to look it up. The issues themselves do not constitute a list of biblical priorities, and the texts only loosely relate to the issues. They do not, for example, deal with the rights of the poor and oppressed, the orphan, the widow or the immigrant, let alone the neighbour. The tenth amendment is revealing. 'We believe in the right of legally-approved religious

organizations to maintain their tax-exempt status, this being based upon
the historical and scriptural concept of church and state separation.'
The proof text is Matthew 22.17–21, a passage which includes the
injunction, 'Render therefore to Caesar the things that are Caesar's, and
to God the things that are God's.' This has normally been taken to mean
that Christians should pay their taxes to Caesar, as the civil power. It is
not clear why the text supports the amendment. Nor is it clear why the
subject is included in the first place. It could be of no concern to the
poor, oppressed, orphans, widows, immigrants or neighbours. In
contrast it was financially crucial for Falwell and the organizations in
which he is involved.

   Jerry Falwell did not always expound the views which are now
associated with the New Right. Prior to that he had a long and
distinguished career as an evangelist, combining deep religious commitment, great personal energy and dynamism, and considerable
organizational flair. He has built up the Thomas Road Baptist Church
in Lynchburg, Virginia, to a congregation of over 17,000. This is a very
considerable achievement, starting as he did thirty years ago with a
congregation of thirty-five, meeting in the former plant of the Donald
Duck Bottling Company.[13] In 1956 he began radio broadcasting, and
later moved into television. His 'Old Time Gospel Hour' is taken by
over 370 television stations, and its mailing list is estimated around three
million. In July 1979 he founded Moral Majority, the most important
body in the New Religious Right. In January of that year Robert Grant
and Richard Zone founded Christian Voice, an organization well-
illustrating the links between the New Right and the New Religious
Right. In 1980 they ran television commercials on behalf of Reagan
against Carter, and targeted some thirty-six congressmen for defeat.
The basis of the judgment on which candidates merited support by
Christians and which did not was the voting records of the Ninety-Sixth
Congress (1979–80). The Congressional Report Card, as it was known,
was sent out to 37,000 pastors and 150,000 lay-people through direct
mailing lists.[14] The issues chosen included sanctions against Rhodesia,
the Taiwan defence treaty, unionization of teachers, school busing,
racial and sexual quotas in school hiring, appropriations to the National
Science Foundation, Salt II, sex education, prayer in schools, abortion,
and private schools. Although some prominent liberal senators on the
list were in fact defeated, including John Culver, George McGovern
and Frank Church, of special interest is the case of Mark Hatfield. As
one of the great liberal voices in the Senate he was targeted for defeat.

He was in fact re-elected, and in a real sense turned the tables on Christian Voice. The Congressional Report Card was intended as a litmus test for the benefit of Christian voters. However, Mark Hatfield is himself a well-known evangelical Christian. The fact that he was targeted became in itself a test of the criteria and commitments of the New Religious Right. Falwell had claimed, 'If a man is not a student of the Word of God and does not know what the Bible says, I question his ability to be an effective leader' (*LA*, 15). Mark Hatfield is such a student of the Word of God, seeking to be faithful to the Bible in the complexities of government. And yet he was targeted. This was an indication that the Report Card identified legislators who were liberals, rather than public figures who were not Christian. Hatfield was well aware of the convolutions. 'They do not bother to ask my view of Jesus Christ in an effort to reach some determination of my salvation: instead they chose to make a judgment on my religious salvation on the basis of my position regarding the Panama Canal Treaty.'[15] As an evangelical Christian sensitive to biblical priorities, Hatfield was critical of the agenda of the New Religious Right. 'Many evangelicals share my concern that the grievous sins of our society are militarism and materialism, rather than the Taiwan Treaty, the Equal Rights Amendment or the Panama Canal.'[16]

It will be clear why the case of Mark Hatfield is so revealing about the true nature of the New Religious Right. If the movement were criticized by liberal Christians this would simply establish its position within the broad conservative spectrum. Such criticisms might even give it status, and on such matters as the inspiration of the Bible could even lead to a defence of the movement by evangelicals. Much more damaging, therefore, are the criticisms of the movement which come from evangelicals. When they declare that the movement is unbiblical, a travesty of Christian faith and responsibility, the New Religious Right is exposed for what it is, an expression of the civil religion of American nationalism tricked out in the language of Old Time Religion. I therefore draw attention to criticisms made not by liberal Christians, but by respected leaders of the evangelical wing. Billy Graham was the most famous evangelist of his time, through the 'Hour of Decision' broadcasts from the early 1950s and his world crusades and missions. Anti-communism was a prominent element in his early work. Later he became closely identified with the Nixon White House. He has certainly not been known as a liberal in social or political matters and at least until his most recent statements probably deserved the assessment by the evangelical writer Jeremy Rifkin, that 'no one dare accuse Graham of being a prophet or a man ahead of his time'.[17] Yet Graham has publicly distanced himself from the New Religious Right. 'I don't wish to be identified with them . . . It would disturb me if there was a wedding between the religious fundamentalists and the political right.'[18] Another rejection comes from Carl Henry, justifiably described as America's leading evangelical theologian. 'The Bible gives no blueprint for a universal evangelical political order. The Moral Majority was misguided by its leaders, who promoted a Christian litmus test of specific issues used to approve or disapprove particular candidates.'[19] No major Christian denomination has associated itself with the movement. Significantly its clerical support comes mainly from independent Baptist ministers. And yet the highly influential and prestigious Southern Baptist Seminary in Louisville, Kentucky, is very critical of the New Religious Right. Among students seventy per cent are opposed to the movement. Professor Paul Simmons identifies aspects to which I have already alluded. 'Civil religion is idolatrous, precisely because it substitutes temporal loyalties for eternal verities. Identifying the Judaeo-Christian posture with American nationalism is to lose the transcendent and absolute nature of the Christian faith.'[20] Those who hold conservative religious positions do not necessarily hold conservative political views. Thus Jim Wallis, a leading young evangelical and member of Sojourners, is much closer to the liberation movements already discussed when he claims that, 'The Bible is clearly and emphatically on the side of the poor, the exploited and the victimized. Nowhere in the Scripture are the rights of the rich proclaimed . . .'[21] Conservatism in religion and politics do not always coincide, but as we have seen, the New Religious Right assimilates the religious to an already established political position. It is this aspect which concerns David Hubbard, President of Fuller Theological Seminary, the leading evangelical school in America. 'I would hate for evangelical Christianity to become a spiritual version of the National Rifle Association.'[22]

Finally I can point, briefly, to a further irony of the New Religious Right. For all its Bible-thumping, it is not Christian: for all its flag-waving, it is not American. Just as in its selection and use of proof texts it fails to perceive the nature of biblical faith, so for all its references to the origins of the Republic, it fails to understand the Constitution. As Samuel Hill observes, 'The flaw in the NRPR (New Religious Political Right) position is that it is not biblical or Constitutional enough.'[23] It has been pointed out that the founding fathers were not all Christian, and that the Constitution guarantees the right of unbelief as well as religious freedom. As Martin Marty observes, 'In effect, the fundamentalist political movement is trying to make second-class citizens of everyone who isn't that, and that the founders deliberately set out not to do it.'[24] Ironically the NRPR (using Hill and Owen's abbreviation) would make second-class citizens of the majority. The problem for moral reformers of societies is that by definition few people accept their views on how they should live their lives. Thus although the reformers must claim they act for the benefit of the majority, they know that they do not have their support. This leads Falwell, for example into a curious position. 'The United States is a republic where laws rule. Although people of the United States have a vote, America is not a democracy in the sense that the majority rules' (*LA*, 15). The founder of Moral Majority is very suspicious of the majority having their way. 'Today we find that America is more of a democracy than a republic. Sometimes there is mob rule' (*LA*, 44). Such sentiments do indeed threaten democracy itself and give substance to the following criticisms by the American Civil Liberties Union. The ACLU claims that 'the new evangelicals are radically anti-Bill of Rights movement'. 'Their kind of "patriotism" violates every principle of liberty that underlies the American system of government.' Instead of being the custodians of the American way, the ACLU describes the movement as tending towards 'religious fascism'. Alternatively they see that 'The New Right, consciously or not, is stealing not only the tactics but the philosophy of Communism.'[25] Notwithstanding the Bible-thumping and the flag-waving, the New Religious Right is neither biblical nor American. The final assessment might go to Paul Simons of the Southern Baptist Seminary. 'It amounts to a coalition of ultra-conservative religion, laissez-faire capitalism and American nationalism. The result is a fervent religious movement that could easily pass for a reactionary political movement. They are equally committed to God, Adam Smith and George Patton – but not necessarily in that order.'[26]

In this chapter we are examining neo-conservative movements which reverse the movement from domination to liberation typical of the 1960s and 1970s. Before the end of the 1970s Senator George McGovern pointed to the change in ethos. 'It is unfashionable now to worry about the poor and minorities and to defend the idea that they, too, deserve an opportunity.'[27] As we have seen, in America this trend to reimpose domination by gender, race and class has sought double legitimation. It has claimed to represent true religion, and also the original spirit of the

nation. But as I have just noted, the movement is neither. To the
contrary, while flourishing the Bible it is profoundly unbiblical, and
while wrapping itself up in the flag, in reality it threatens to destroy the
nation. We must not assume that neo-conservatism, in America or in
Britain, is the true custodian either of the religious life or the well-being
of the nation. Richard Viguerie has included sixteen pages of informal
photographs in his book. Among the white faces, he is seen with Jerry
Falwell and also with President Ronald Reagan. Barry Goldwater and
William Buckley Jr are included, as is Milton Friedman. Only one non-
American appears in what is for the most part an image-reinforcing
exercise, and that is Margaret Thatcher. This seems entirely appropriate. When she came to power in 1979 she was determined to make a
break with old-style conservatism. In order to formulate her alternative
she borrowed extensively from the New Right in America. Although the
specific issues might be different, the objective was the same, to replace
the new consensus of the 1960s and 1970s with a neo-conservative
ethos.

When I was an economics student I recall a series of lectures on the
nationalized industries in which an ingenious but elegant theory was
propounded concerning importing and exporting of coal. The lectures
were given in November. All the conditions favouring the theory
unexpectedly came about in May. The lecturer suddenly reappeared
just before the university examinations to explain why it was that, even
so, the theory did not work. It was about that time that I noticed that all
economists have two hands. Economics is far from being an exact
science. This is no reflection on economists, but a consequence of the
number of variables, principally human behaviour, constituent of the
subject. It is therefore surprising that neo-conservative governments
should put such faith in economics and economists. The word 'faith' is
used here deliberately, because on closer inspection it becomes clear
that economics is invested with moral properties or at the very least is
assumed to serve a moral order. The dimension of faith in neo-
conservatism does not refer to the gap between theory and outcome,
which prevents economics from being an exact science, but rather to the
gap between economic policies and the moral values which are assumed
inherent within them. If I say that neo-conservatism pins its faith on
economics, I do not mean that it is hoping against hope that this useful
tool (some would think it closer to the chisel end of the precision
spectrum rather than the scalpel end) will do the job. The dimension of
faith lies in the assumption that there are moral values within economics

such that by implementing certain economic policies, particular moral goals will be realized. The view is not of course new. It is significant that in Glasgow Adam Smith, the founding father of Political Economy in the eighteenth century, occupied the chair of Moral Philosophy. He believed in a natural order within which the pursuit of private interest tended towards the achievement of public good. 'Herein lies the *a priori* element in Adam Smith; there is a natural order, appointed by a wise Providence, in which self-interest will supply the necessary drive to make the machine go, and will also so act as to produce equilibrium between contending forces. This leads to what is in the main a wholly optimistic view of a world in which a beneficent deity has arranged that progress and harmony shall result from the free-play of instincts which are, frankly, self-centred and self-concerned.'[28] This view, or a variation on it, has been revived in recent times. It is not a position which flows directly from religious faith, but a particular extrapolation. And apparently in more secular times it can be held even without belief in Providence. In this case, however, the view, now a moral philosophy rather than a theological doctrine, would require a great deal of work to provide its justification. In these circumstances religious legitimation would be of considerable assistance. By way of digression we might point out that this is one of those places where political left and right come close. Both left and right secularize the belief in Providence. Thus when neo-conservatives claim that certain economic relationships will achieve desirable moral goals both for individuals and for society as a whole, they are in agreement with a fundamental premise of Marx's historical materialism. The agreement is not that economic policies can be made to serve moral goals, but that certain economic relationships are themselves inherently moral. Naturally the agreement ends there. To 'unbelievers' both approaches might lack credibility – however, they might approve of the moral values involved. Yet because both positions originally derive from a doctrine of providence, they have a family resemblance with religion and can attract religious legitimation from those who hold the particular values advocated. For example it would be comforting to be able to pursue self-interest with a good heart and clear conscience, not because we shall reap economic benefits but because we shall automatically assist the poorer members of society. And if there is not a scrap of evidence to support such an economic theory, it could still be pursued by faith if we came to believe that God's invisible hand so arranged things. And those who accept the theory but do not have religious faith can be encouraged by the religious legitimation offered by otherwise like-minded people. Now as we turn to consider the situation in Britain we must examine the extent to which neo-conservatism turns away from liberation towards relationships which reassert domination by gender, race and class, and the extent to which it is offered religious legitimation.

Sir Keith Joseph will be remembered as a politician who broke new ground. He is credited with doing more than any Secretary of State before him to run down education in Britain at both higher and tertiary levels. However, his more lasting contribution to political life is that he is said to have created Thatcherism. He formulated and proclaimed neo-conservatism towards the end of the 1970s when it was fashionable neither in the country at large nor even within the Conservative Party. Two points which were later to become central appear in the following statement published in 1979, the year of the election which brought Mrs Thatcher to power. 'There have been some stout defences of private enterprise, though few of them have met the arguments on moral grounds, and it has been the arguments from moral premises which have been most telling. The reason for the Conservative Party's inability to mount a sufficiently robust defence of free enterprise is that the Conservative Party is not, by nature, a party of ideology.'[29] Sir Keith is referring to the attacks on capitalism throughout the period of the 1960s and 1970s. They were not concerned with efficiency, but with justice: wealth for some has brought woe for many. In calling for a new defence of capitalism he is claiming that economic arguments will not win the day. Indeed those who are content with economic arguments will convey an impression of indifference to the morality of the issues. Capitalism must now be promoted on moral as well as economic grounds. The second point concerns ideology. While it is true that the High Toryism to which I referred at the outset was thoroughly pragmatic and had no interest in ideology, neo-conservatism has constructed and promoted an ideology. It has produced an account of the social world which identifies values and goals, which brings forward analyses and explanations of why things are as they are and require to be changed. And in common with all ideological faiths, it is impervious to facts. Toryism was pragmatic. There was nothing at stake if policies had to be changed. But an ideological faith cannot afford to admit the facts because the whole edifice would collapse. For policies ruled by facts there are always alternatives. Policies which arise from an ideological faith cannot be changed without undermining the premises upon which the whole system is constructed. The strident insistence that THERE IS NO

ALTERNATIVE is symptomatic that we are in the presence of ideological faith. Such a faith must claim the higher moral ground. Neo-conservatism is therefore an ideology promoted in face of facts: its policies are working, though unemployment is now out of control. It is an ideological faith which claims to be promoting good even when many experience it as evil. In the economic sphere the patient died, but the operation was successful. In the moral sphere the patient died but the treatment was for his own good. No one could be converted to policies which had such devastating effects, but many have been converted to the ideological faith which justifies them. As Sir Keith says, 'There is now the beginnings of real defence of private enterprise – based on social, political and moral, as well as economic grounds.'[30]

These words were published in the Foreword entitled 'In Defence of Free Enterprise' which Sir Keith wrote for a collection of essays on *The Case for Private Enterprise*. Even in 1979 he observes that it can no longer be assumed that every politically literate person under twenty-five is a socialist. He looks forward to a new generation who will argue for capitalism with all the fervour of a moral campaign. This is illustrated in the first essay in the volume, 'The Moral Case for Private Enterprise', by Chris Tame. I have already noted that when neo-conservatism first appeared it had no ideological tradition behind it, and borrowed extensively from a similar movement which was already developing in America. Tame, previously head of the research department of the National Association for Freedom, takes as a motto for his essay a quotation from the American philosopher Ayn Rand: 'The New Intellectuals must fight for capitalism, not as a "practical" issue, not as an economic issue, but with the most righteous pride, as a *moral* issue. That is what capitalism deserves, and nothing less will save it.'[31] These words, written twenty-five years ago, are a prophetic rallying call to the new faith. Such conviction economics makes a strong appeal, as it combines three distinct elements. At a psychological level it calls for single-minded devotion to a cause. At a moral level it requires a commitment to a righeous path. And at the level of human nature it offers the prospect of material advantage for the individual. Unlike most moral philosophies and all higher religions, conviction economics believes that its brand of morality brings a healthy profit in this life. As already noted earlier, this proposition might seem to most people totally unfounded. It would require a metaphysical faith which was prepared to offer explanations in particular cases of why morality and reward are not linked. But Tame is not offering such a system. He is confident that looking out for yourself brings rewards. Now *that* is a proposition with which most people could agree. The difficulty arises when such an attitude is called moral. Tame therefore bites the bullet and advocates 'ethical egoism'.[32] He acknowledges that the common theme in most criticisms of private enterprise and the free market is 'that of the *moral evil* of private ownership, the profit motive, and 'selfish' private enterprise'.[33] It could be argued that from its origins socialism has been an ethical system, with economic consequences. Thus for socialists a certain inefficiency might be reckoned the acceptable cost of producing a humane society. In Tame's view the opposite would be true of capitalism. Although it did not set out to be a moral system, it has been discovered that its relationships embody and promote moral values and consequently produce a humane society. The outside observer might remain sceptical of both sides, but it is in this context that Tame sees the alternatives as constituting 'a moral dichotomy'.[34] In presenting capitalism as a moral system Tame is borrowing something from Adam Smith, and more recently from the American New Right, notably George Gilder, to whom I have previously referred: the profit motive requires that the entrepreneur serves others in the market place. (They also gain, who only stand and serve.) All credit to Tame, he does not fudge the critical issue. 'For it is precisely the "selfishness" of private enterprise that constitutes its moral virtue, its *moral* glory.'[35] No one could accuse him of soft-sell or under-stating his case.

Neo-conservatism therefore seeks legitimation by two different routes. The first is that it is presented as an ideological faith. This means that it is incorrigible by facts. Evidence which disproves its theories can be interpreted or explained to the satisfaction of believers. The second route is that of conviction economics, that it is morally justified to pursue self-interest, from which will accrue benefits both to the individual taking the initiative and to society generally. I have previously noted that this faith in a moral order is something which the ideological Right shares with the ideological Left. However, the content of the moral order is quite different. Neo-conservatism is sometimes analysed together with neo-liberalism[36] and no doubt there is a connection with nineteenth-century liberalism and the protection of rights which belonged to the middle classes, but in respect of the moral issue it is more instructive to look to Nietzsche and the development of fascism. The cultural crisis as Nietzsche discerned it just over a century ago lay in the moral values which had permeated European culture through Christianity. Such virtues as pity and compassion he thought inhibited the will to power, the single-minded drive of the supermen who could transcend the ethos of passivity and acceptance. Nietzsche therefore set out to effect a 'transvaluation of all values'. He saw himself standing in the Renaissance tradition: 'The revaluation of Christian values, the atempt, undertaken with every expedient, with every instinct, with genius of every kind, to bring about the victory of the opposing values, the *noble* values.'[37] Those who wish to advocate 'ethical egoism' must undertake a comparable transvaluation of values. They must convince people that the traditional virtues are quite misguided, and that it is their moral duty to espouse quite different values. But, as Nietzsche saw, Christian moral teaching stands in the way of such a change. What neo-conservatism requires is therefore a reinterpretation of Christianity, which demonstrates that properly understood Christianity really teaches ethical egoism. But who will undertake this reinterpretation? Few theologians deal with Christian social teaching, and perhaps none who do would accept the premises of the argument. There is, however, a possible solution. In the free market world of neo-conservatism restrictive practices in the professions are being dismantled. Thus banks are now competing with building societies, building societies with lawyers, and lawyers with banks. In the same spirit of free enterprise why should not a conviction economist provide the reinterpretation of religion required for the legitimation of ethical egoism? And in keeping with the new supply side ethos, no sooner is the need identified than the service is offered.

Brian Griffiths, Dean of the City University Business School, London, begins his discussion of 'Christianity and Capitalism' (= *C & C*) [38] with two quotations from José Miguez Bonino which typify the view of Latin American theologians that capitalism is incompatible with Christianity. Griffiths maintains that the market economy has transformed Western economies and brought not only wealth, but a spread of wealth throughout society. Third World countries which have followed this example have enjoyed economic growth unparalleled among those which have practised state planning. However, economic growth would not be a sufficient argument, he claims, if it did not also raise general standards of living and eliminate absolute poverty. Presumably these considerations come close to the moral dimensions of the issue. Griffiths would argue that for those concerned to alleviate or eliminate poverty, the economic development of market economies has not caused the poverty of other countries, nor would the world problem be addressed by a redistribution of capital which would destroy the productive base of the market economies without providing a long-term solution. 'Indeed, by breeding dependence on handouts, the redistribution of wealth through the coercive power of the state can make matters worse' (*C & C*, 106). This is a line of argument we have encountered in the American context, expressed there as a preference for charity over welfare. Griffiths now moves to his more specific subject. How can the market economy be accepted in terms of efficiency and morality, if it is incompatible with Christian principles? 'Much more difficult is the apparent inconsistency between the teachings of Jesus and the apostles and the very principles on which the market economy depends for success' (*C & C*, 107). Griffiths brushes aside too quickly 'the early Church's first short-lived experiment with communism'. It is surely of some significance that the first initiative the followers of Jesus took was to form such a community. Presumably it continued an experience they had had with Jesus. Its theological significance has never been seriously pursued, though it has always remained a powerful ideal down through the centuries for Christians who wished to establish a life-style based on Christian values. The fact that Christians are indistinguishable from their neighbours in economic matters cannot be a matter of indifference in view of the radical teaching of Jesus, nor can this conformity to social norms be seen in itself as adequate theological grounds for dismissing the actions of the followers of Jesus who in so many other areas are regarded as authoritative.

Griffiths prefers to begin not with the New Testament, but with the Old. In fairness we must admit that in the Old Testament we find principles enunciated for the guidance of the life of a small nation, while in the New Testament the small ecclesial communities have virtually no impact on the life of the Roman empire. It is tempting therefore to look to the documents which deal with national life. The books of the Hebrew Scriptures were not written in the order in which they now appear, which means that their present order has profound theological significance. God is first encountered as Creator, and men and women made in His image presumably are also to be creative. They are given dominion over the material world, though domination either of nature or of each other is a consequence of the Fall. Man's relationship to the natural world also suffers in consequence. 'Poverty, famine and misery are not part of the Creator's intention for the world' (*C & C*, 108). Griffiths therefore addresses two elements in the contemporary debate. One is the tendency for many in industrial societies to view economic activity as an inferior way of life. The other is the existence of suffering in the world. 'The challenge for the Christian then is not to reject the material world and the business of wealth creation in favour of some higher spiritual priority, but to serve others through the process of wealth creation in the process of serving God' (*C & C*, 108). These are worthy religious sentiments, though neither aspect has anything to do with Genesis. The quotation is a good example of eisegesis, reading views back into the text. It sets an interesting agenda, but it leaves wide open the question whether wealth creation (market economy) is a way of serving God, and whether the process deserves the religious connotations of the phrase 'to serve others'. We should have to say that Griffiths is making the now familiar assumption that as I pursue my interests, I serve God and incidentally serve my neighbour as well. This scenario seems unlikely, and there is nothing in Genesis to suggest otherwise.

Griffiths now turns to a second issue in the debate about capitalism, namely the question of private property. He clearly wishes to head off any thought of redistribution of land. But although this is a contemporary issue in some countries it was not in ancient Israel. As Griffiths notes, the problem was the accumulation of property in the hands of a few. There was, however, an egalitarian ethos in the earlier periods which is not at all what Griffiths wishes to find. This element has been pointed out by Werner Schmidt. 'There were indeed certain social safeguards and legal prescriptions that sought to maintain the economic and social equality of the members of the people of God, and in fact these probably worked for a time.'[39] Griffiths points to the Jubilee, the handing back of land in the fiftieth year and the cancellation of debts.[40] To this Schmidt adds the injunction against charging interest. It would be as well for the advocates of the free market to cut their losses at this point and argue that these rules were for a primitive pre-industrial economy and are not applicable for modern times. But if they wish to gain support from the Bible for their position would they not be faced with the possibility that these Levitical laws might apply to many Third World countries today?

A third issue concerns economic justice in the period of the classical prophets. Griffiths takes comfort from the thought that when the prophets criticized the rich for exploiting the poor, 'yet they never suggested that the remedy was therefore a redistribution of wealth undertaken in some sort of religious vacuum' (*C & C*, 109). But to make this the only criterion is a culpable misreading of the texts. Here is the well known passage from Amos, who describes what the exercise of freedom amounts to in the free market economy.

Hear this, you who trample upon the needy,
and bring the poor of the land to an end,
saying, 'When will the new moon be over,
that we may sell grain?
And the sabbath,
that we may offer wheat for sale,
that we may make the ephah small and the shekel great,
and deal deceitfully with false balances,
that we may buy the poor for silver
and the needy for a pair of sandals,
and sell the refuse of the wheat?'   (Amos 8.4–6).

No, the eighth-century prophets did not advocate state planning, but they spoke God's condemnation upon the way in which the free market operated. In an evil and manifestly unequal world, simply to advocate freedom is to issue licences for exploitation. It is interesting to see that Griffiths would like the material from the Old Testament to support an entirely different conclusion.

> From those Old Testament attitudes to the material world, property and justice – assumed by Jesus in all his teaching – a number of principles emerge. Private property rather than social ownership of wealth and the means of production is the norm. Permanent access by each family to a stake in economic life is guaranteed. And some form of anti-poverty programme is written into the laws to ensure just and compassionate treatment for the economically weak. In all this there is nothing to suggest that the basic institutions of Western economies are incompatible with a Christian world view (*C & C*, 109–10).

But can legislation for welfare and the denunciation of the free market really be taken as a biblical defence of capitalism? And all this without so much as a mention of the hard words of Jesus. 'Blessed are you poor, for yours is the kingdom of God' (Luke 6.21). The ministry of Jesus is the fulfilment of the prophecy of Isaiah: 'The Spirit of the Lord is upon me, because he has anointed me to preach good news to the poor.' What can this be but that their poverty is to end? 'For where your treasure is, there will your heart be also' (Matthew 6.21). 'You cannot serve God and mammon' (Matthew 6.24) 'You lack one thing; go sell what you have, and give to the poor, and you will have treasure in heaven; and come, follow me' (Mark 10.21). 'For it is easier for a camel to go through the eye of a needle than for a rich man to enter the kingdom of God' (Luke

18.25). These are hard words (and there are many more) not simply because they would be hard to comply with, but because it is difficult to see how they could begin to deal with the problem of poverty. Would it not be morally irresponsible for a father, in respect of his children, or in this case an employer with respect to his employees, to 'take therefore no thought for the morrow' (AV/KJV Matthew 6.34)? But however we wrestle with these hard words, surely they cannot be taken as a straightforward endorsement of capitalism.

Having given the impression that he has cleared away the matter of whether capitalism is compatible with Christianity, Griffiths now turns to the moral criticisms of the market economy. He takes up the accusations that it is a system founded upon greed and self-interest, that it is entirely guided by the profit motive, and that it is synonymous with selfishness. There are further criticisms that it is a system which manufactures inequality, and fosters individualism. His approach in general can be seen from the following statement. 'It is not the environment that determines the morality of behaviour but the individual making the decisions' (*C & C*, 110). There is here the same naivety which we encountered in the earlier chapters when dealing with domination. Then we saw that the most profound and disturbing feature was that within a system built on domination, even well-intentioned people dominate others. We saw that the injustice of the system could not be attributed to malevolence. Indeed the situation was such that an inherently dominating system dominated more efficiently precisely when it was operated by people of good character and great integrity. If so then it is quite naive to think that the market economy can be moral if only individual entrepreneurs are moral. 'Similarly a businessman committed to certain moral principles can actively seek the welfare of his staff and clients in the context of his commercial activities' (*C & C*, 110). Capitalism as an economic system is founded on domination and cannot operate without domination. And as with other comparable systems, the domination is not a result of any intention on the part of individuals who operate it. The corollary is that neither can it cease to dominate when operated by people who are otherwise well-disposed towards the unemployed in this country and the poor of the Third World. Neo-conservatism seeks to give free rein to the market economy, and this means that those who are most vulnerable will experience renewed domination – domination by gender, race and class. But domination can no longer count on legitimation from the followers of Christ the Liberator.

Notes

Introduction

1. Theo Witvliet, *A Place in the Sun: An Introduction to Liberation Theology in the Third World*, SCM Press and Orbis Books, Maryknoll 1985, p. 148.
2. Allan Boesak, *Black Theology and Black Power*, Mowbrays 1978, p. 143.
3. Carter Heyward, 'An Unfinished Symphony of Liberation: The Radicalization of Christian Feminism Among White US Women', *Journal of Feminist Studies in Religion*, Vol. 1, No. 1, Spring 1985, p. 101.
4. Peter Berger, *The Social Reality of Religion*, Penguin Books 1973, p. 41.
5. Quoted by Martin Marty. See Peggy L. Shriver, *The Bible Vote*, Pilgrim Press, New York 1981, p. 38.
6. Richard Shaull, 'Foreword' to Rubem A. Alves, *Protestantism and Repression*, Orbis Books, Maryknoll and SCM Press 1985, p. xvii.

1. Religion and the Domination of Women

1. Betty Friedan, *The Feminine Mystique*, Penguin Books 1965.
2. Simone de Beauvoir, *The Second Sex*, Penguin Books 1972 (French original 1949).
3. Kate Millett, *Sexual Politics*, Abacus 1972.
4. Phyllis Bird, 'Images of Women in the Old Testament', in Rosemary Radford Ruether (ed.), *Religion and Sexism*, Simon & Schuster, New York 1974, pp. 41–88.
5. Elisabeth Schüssler Fiorenza, *In Memory of Her*, Crossroad Publishing Co and SCM Press 1983.
6. The following examples are taken from the typical quotations gathered in feminist studies of misogyny in Greek sources and in the fathers of the church. See especially Nancy van Vuuren, *The Subversion of Women*, Westminster Press, Philadelphia 1973; Mary Briody Mahowald (ed.), *Philosophy of Women*, Hackett Publishing Co., Indianapolis 1978; Denise C. Hogan, *Woman and the Christian Experience*, PhD Dissertation, Boston University Graduate School 1975; chapters by Rosemary Radford Ruether, Constance F. Parvey and Eleanor Commo McLaughlin in *Religion and Sexism*.
7. Elisabeth Moltmann-Wendel, *Humanity in God*, Pilgrim Press, New York and SCM Press, 1984.
8. Karl Marx, 'Contribution to the Critique of Hegel's Philosophy of Law: Introduction', Karl Marx and Frederick Engels, *Collected Works*, Vol. 3, Lawrence and Wishart 1975, p. 182.
9. In Ruether (ed.), *Sexism and Religion*.
10. Rosemary Radford Ruether, *Sexism and God-Talk*, Beacon Press, Boston

and SCM Press 1983, p. 194.
11. Alistair Kee (ed.), *The Scope of Political Theology*, SCM Press 1978, p. 65.
12. *The Regulation of Birth*, Catholic Truth Society 1968.

2. *The Power of the Black Jesus*

1. Albert Cleage, *The Black Messiah*, Sheed & Ward 1968, p. 37.
2. James Cone, *Black Theology and Black Power*, Seabury Press, New York 1969, p. 38.
3. Stokely Carmichael and Charles V. Hamilton, *Black Power*, Penguin Books 1969, p. 52.
4. Karl Barth, *Church Dogmatics*, T. & T. Clark 1957, Vol. II.1, p. 635.
5. J. Deotis Roberts, *A Black Political Theology*, Westminster Press, Philadelphia 1974, p. 208.
6. Johannes B. Metz, *Theology of the World*, Herder & Herder, New York 1969, p. 109.
7. Tissa Balasuriya, *Planetary Theology*, Orbis Books, Maryknoll and SCM Press 1984, p. 117. See also his *The Eucharist and Human Liberation*, Orbis Books, Maryknoll and SCM Press 1979.
8. Allan Aubrey Boesak, *Black Theology/Black Power*, Mowbrays 1978.
9. Carter Heyward, 'An Unfinished Symphony of Liberation: The Radicalization of Christian Feminism Among White US Women', *Journal of Feminist Studies in Religion*, Vol. 1, No. 1, Spring 1985, p. 101.

3. *Marx and Liberation Theology*

1. Karl Marx, *Capital: A Critique of Political Economy*, Penguin Books 1976, Vol. 1, Postface to Second Edition, 1873, p. 103.
2. *Marx-Engels Werke*, quoted by José Porfirio Miranda, *Marx Against the Marxists*, Orbis Books, Maryknoll and SCM Press 1980, p. 246.
3. Ibid., p. 251.
4. Ibid., p. 241.
5. Ludwig Feuerbach, *The Essence of Christianity*, reissued Harper & Row, New York 1957, pp. 29–30.
6. Karl Marx and Frederick Engels, *Collected Works*, Lawrence & Wishart 1975, Vol. 3, p. 175.
7. Loc. cit.
8. Loc. cit.
9. Karl Marx, *Early Writings*, translated and edited by T. B. Bottomore, C. A. Watts & Co. 1963, p. 44.
10. Ibid., p. 37.
11. Ibid., p. 167.
12. Karl Marx, *Early Writings*, Penguin Books 1975, p. 241.
13. Quoted in Miranda, *Marx Against the Marxists*, p. 280.
14. Quoted in A. H. Armstrong, *An Introduction to Ancient Philosophy*, Methuen 1968 (1947), p. 23.

15. G. W. F. Hegel, *Philosophy of Right*, Oxford University Press 1952, Preface, p. 10.

16. Karl Marx, *Early Writings*, p. 423.

17. Jon Sobrino, *The True Church and the Poor*, Orbis Books, Maryknoll and SCM Press 1985, p. 16.

18. Karl Marx and Frederick Engels, *The German Ideology*, Lawrence & Wishart 1970, Part I, p. 47.

19. Ibid., p. 64.

20. Julio de Santa Ana, *Good News to the Poor*, World Council of Churches, Geneva 1977, p. 2.

21. Sobrino, *TC*, 2. Compare David Sheppard, *Bias to the Poor*, Hodder and Stoughton 1983.

22. José Miranda, *Marx and the Bible*, Orbis Books, Maryknoll and SCM Press 1974, p. 57.

23. Quoted by Alfredo Fierro, *The Militant Gospel*, Orbis Books, Maryknoll and SCM Press 1977, p. 197.

24. The full text of the document was published in *The Tablet*, 8 September 1984, pp. 868–74.

25. Leonardo Boff, *Church, Charism and Power*, Crossroad Publishing Co and SCM Press 1985.

26. For a detailed comparison of the Instruction and Boff's book see my article 'Authority and Liberation: Conflict Between Rome and Latin America', *The Modern Churchman*, NS Vol. XXVIII No. 1, 1985, pp. 27–35.

27. Karl Marx, 'The Critique of Hegel's Philosophy of Right: Introduction', *Early Writings* (Bottomore), p. 58.

28. Karl Marx and Frederick Engels, *Selected Works*, Lawrence & Wishart 1970, p. 182.

29. Ibid., p. 181.

30. Ernst Troeltsch, *The Social Teaching of the Christian Churches*, Lutterworth Press and Harper & Brothers, New York 1960, Vol. I, p. 63.

4. The New Religious Right

1. Rubem A. Alves, *Protestantism and Repression: A Brazilian Case Study*, Orbis Books, Maryknoll and SCM Press 1985 (original 1979).

2. Rubem A. Alves, *A Theology of Human Hope*, Corpus Books, New York 1969; *Tomorrow's Child*, SCM Press 1972.

3. Karl Marx and Frederick Engels, *The German Ideology*, p. 47.

4. Karl Marx, 'The Critique of Hegel's Philosophy of Right: Introduction', *Early Writings* (Bottomore), p. 44.

5. See Sydney E. Mead, 'The "Nation with the Soul of a Church"', *Church History* 36 (Sept. 1967), pp. 262–83, reprinted in Russell E, Richey and Donal C. Jones (eds.) *Civil Religion*, Harper & Row, New York 1974.

6. Jerry Falwell, *Listen America!*, Bantam Books, New York 1981, pp. 7–8.

7. Jean-Jacques Rousseau, *The Social Contract and Discourses*, J. M. Dent & Sons Ltd. 1973, p. 272.

8. Quoted by Robert B. Bellah in 'Civil Religion in America', *Daedalus*

(Winter) 1967, reprinted in Robert N. Bellah, *Beyond Belief*, Harper & Row 1970, p. 175.

9. Richard A. Viguerie, *The New Right – We're Ready to Lead*, The Viguerie Company, Falls Church, Va. 1981.

10. *US News & World Report*, July 1977, quoted by Viguerie, p. 62.

11. Robert N. Bellah, 'The New Religious Consciousness and the Crisis in Modernity', in Charles Y. Glock and Robert N. Bellah (eds.), *The New Religious Consciousness*, University of California Press, Berkeley 1976, pp. 333–52.

12. Robert Sherrill et al. *Governing America*, Harcourt, Brace, Jovanovich 1978, p. 52.

13. Robert C. Liebman, 'Mobilizing the Moral Majority', in Robert C. Liebman and Robert Withnow (eds.), *The New Christian Right: Mobilization and Legitimation*, Aldine Publishing Company, New York 1983, p. 58.

14. Ibid., p. 53.

15. Quoted in Peggy L. Shriver, *The Bible Vote: Religion and the New Right*, The Pilgrim Press, New York 1981, p. 74.

16. Ibid., p. 142.

17. Jeremy Rifkin, *The Emerging Order: God in the Age of Scarcity*, Ballantine Books, New York 1979, p. 158.

18. Quoted in Samuel S. Hill and Dennis E. Owen, *The New Religious Political Right in America*, Abingdon Press, Nashville 1982, pp. 16–17.

19. Quoted ibid., pp. 84–5.

20. Quoted ibid., p. 88.

21. Quoted Rifkin, p. 165.

22. Quoted Shriver, p. 82.

23. Hill and Owen, p. 40.

24. Quoted Shriver, p. 62.

25. Quoted by James Davison Hunter, 'The Liberal Reaction', in Liebman and Wuthnow, pp. 155–6.

26. Quoted in Hill and Owen, p. 88.

27. Quoted Rifkin, p. 5.

28. Alexander Gray, *The Development of Economic Doctrine*, Longmans, Green & Co. 1951, p. 125.

29. Sir Keith Joseph, 'In Defence of Free Enterprise', Foreword to Cecil Turner (ed.), *The Case for Private Enterprise*, Bachman & Turner Ltd, 1979, p. 11.

30. Ibid., p. 12.

31. Ayn Rand, *For the New Intellectual*, New American Library, New York 1961. Quoted in Turner, p. 17.

32. Ibid., p. 26.

33. Ibid., p. 17.

34. Ibid., p. 23.

35. Loc. cit.

36. Ruth Levitas (ed.), *The Ideology of the New Right*, Polity Press, Cambridge 1986, pp. 3ff.

37. Friedrich Nietzsche, *The Anti-Christ* (and *Twilight of the Idols*), Penguin Books 1971 (original 1895), p. 184.

38. Brian Griffiths, 'Christianity and Capitalism', in Digby Anderson (ed.),

The Kindness that Kills: The Churches' Simplistic Response to Complex Social Issues.
SPCK 1984.

39. Werner H. Schmidt, *Introduction to the Old Testament*, Crossroad
Publishing Co., New York and SCM Press 1984, pp. 36–7.

40. Leviticus 25.